Teacher, Guide, Companion

Teacher, Guide, Companion

Rediscovering Jesus in a Secular World

Erik Walker Wikstrom

SKINNER HOUSE BOOKS
BOSTON

Printed in Canada.

Cover design by Kathryn Sky-Peck

ISBN 1-55896-458-4

Library of Congress Cataloging-in-Publication Data

Wikstrom, Erik Walker.
    Teacher, guide, companion : rediscovering Jesus in a secular world / Erik Walker Wikstrom.
        p.cm.
    Includes bibliographical references.
    ISBN 1-55896-458-4 (alk. paper)
    1. Spiritual life—Christianity. 2. Jesus Christ—Person and offices. 3. Bible. N.T. Gospels—Criticism, interpretation, etc. I. Title.

BV4501.3.W5425 2003
232—dc21   2003045513

5 4 3 2 1
06 05 04 03

The Scripture quotations contained herein are from the New Revised Standard Version Bible, copyright © 1989 by the Division of Christian Education of the National Council of the Churches of Christ in the U.S.A., and are used by permission. All rights reserved. Gospel of Thomas quotations are from *The Five Gospels: What Did Jesus Really Say?* with new translation and commentary by Robert W. Funk, Roy W. Hoover, and the Jesus Seminar. Polebridge Press, 1993.

.

To my mother, Nancy Haney Wikstrom,
who told me that I would one day rediscover Jesus,
and to my best friend and life partner, Mary Brand-James,
without whom nothing would be possible.

You search the scriptures because you think that in them you have eternal life; and it is they that bear witness to me; yet you refuse to come to me that you may have life.

— *John 5:39–40*

Split a piece of wood; I am there. Lift up the stone, and you will find me there.

—*Thomas 77:2–3*

Contents

Foreword

I REMEMBER A MINISTERS' CONVOCATION many years ago with the usual full assembly of distinguished lecturers and a designated and prestigious preacher. The worship was rich. The preacher was dazzling. He preached out of his tradition and out of the power he felt in following Jesus as his Lord and Savior. This preacher was compelling. I felt myself drawn into his words. And then he moved out of the pulpit and came around to the communion table in the front. On this table stood a bronze cross. The preacher was near the end of his sermon, and his voice was reaching a crescendo. "It is as if Jesus is alive in this moment," he cried, "separated only by the flash of the generations. Imagine you are in the periphery of this great crowd across time, standing on the shoulders of your forebears, and Jesus is calling out to you, 'Follow me!'" And then the preacher touched the cross with one hand and with the other he touched someone in the front row.

I remember going home that day thinking, "This is dangerous stuff." I could imagine hearing a voice like that inviting me to follow, and then what would I do? There was an instant that afternoon when I would have followed: just picked up a few things, left all the rest behind and followed. It was a close call. I remember going to school in the South and hearing Sunday night Gospel radio and powerful preaching, always ending with a fervent plea for financial support. I'd write the check before going to bed, and I'd tear it up in the light of morning. Another close call.

Taking Jesus seriously has always meant for me a kind of personal surrender, but that says more about me than it says about Jesus. Somewhere in my spiritual odyssey, I moved into that dichotomy that either Jesus is the exclusive way to God or he isn't. I fell for the passage in which Jesus is supposed to have said, "No one comes to the Father but by me," and I decided that wouldn't do. In fact, somewhere along the way a "belief" in Jesus became an embarrassment. When I was young, Jesus was good enough. But I remember thinking to myself somewhere along the way, "I've moved beyond that now." To hear someone claim his or her faith with the words "we see the light and you don't" only pushed me away.

I now serve a Unitarian Universalist congregation that has more than a handful of members who may have been wounded by the church of their upbringing. In my own congregation, I have people who count the number of times I say "God" or "Jesus" during the worship hour, and I have people who notice when I do not.

Erik's book was written for people like me. This book is an invitation, pure and simple. Are we willing to take a fresh look at a relationship that we thought we had left behind or that we had left because of irreconcilable differences, and we had settled for being "just friends" with Jesus? I think Erik is right when he says this book "is not for the faint-hearted." For me, it goes back to that afternoon when the preacher touched the cross and tried to touch me. There is power in that kind of connection, and I have found I am ready to open the conversation again, to take a new look at my relationship with Jesus. Erik's spiritual journey is enough like my own, and he expresses himself in such an honest way, that I am willing to let him be my guide.

Rev. Gary E. Smith
September, 2003

Introduction

Do not be frightened from this inquiry by any fear of its consequences. . . . You must lay aside all prejudices on both sides,
and neither believe nor reject anything, because any other persons, or descriptions of persons, have rejected or believed it.
Your own reason is the only oracle given you by heaven.

—Thomas Jefferson, letter to Peter Carr, August 10, 1787

HE LIVED OVER TWO THOUSAND YEARS AGO in a small town in a back-
water province. He spent his entire life in an area slightly smaller
than the state of Vermont. He never appeared on television. He
never wrote a book. Yet this Jewish peasant—born to unwed teen-
age parents—continues to fascinate people, believers and nonbe-
lievers alike. Who was he? What are we to make of the claims
made on his behalf? And what, if anything, does it mean in the
twenty-first century to profess to have a relationship with him?

I first encountered Jesus when I was a child. I'm not sure what
my Sunday School teachers intended for me to learn, but I can
remember the image I formed of Him (in those days, always a
capital "H"). He was white (like me) and had brown hair, which
was long, straight, and impeccably groomed, as was the beard that

covered his thin (nearly gaunt) face. His teeth were white and perfect; his eyes were a piercing blue and a little sad. His body was thin and wiry; his hands were soft and his fingers long. He wore a white robe that covered him down to his sandled feet.

The Jesus of my childhood spoke softly, moved gracefully, and was always calm and gentle. He never raised his voice and never had negative feelings like anger, fear, jealousy, or self-doubt. He never even had a negative thought. Pure in word and deed, he was "perfect, as [his] Heavenly Father was perfect" (Matthew 5:48). He always knew the right thing to do and did it without hesitation. He was kind and good, compassionate to all, yet detached, unearthly. Jesus was something more than human. Jesus was held up to me as a role model, yet I knew his was a role no one else could ever hope to play. I knew that I, at least, would never be good enough.

This Sunday School image remained essentially unquestioned even when I had stopped believing in its literal truth. In some ways it's with me still: Jesus, the perfect man, the saint, the God-man. Even when I came to question everything else about his story, this Sunday School image continued to influence my thinking. This was the first Jesus I ever knew.

I encountered Jesus again when I was an older youth. The musical Godspell and the rock opera Jesus Christ, Superstar brought an entirely new Jesus to light—a Jesus who laughed and got angry, a Jesus who doubted and made mistakes. (During this time some of the elevated reverence would fade; I stopped thinking of him, for instance, with a capital "H.") I read Nikos Kazantzakis' book The Last Temptation of Christ, in which I encountered a Jesus who was not God, who was instead a tool of God, an instrument of the divine will. And Kazantzakis' Jesus was not a willing instrument either. This was a thoroughly human Jesus who so desperately wanted to avoid his sacred destiny that, as a young man, he sought to offend God by using his carpenter's skills to make the crosses on which the Romans were crucifying zealot Jews. Surely some-thing so horrendous would make God give up on him. It didn't, of course, and the story unfolds in both familiar and surprising ways. This was a different Jesus than I had met before.

Looking back at the Gospel stories from this perspective, I found new meaning in what I had learned is the shortest verse of the Bible, John 11:35, "Jesus wept." Jesus was no impassive saint! I rediscov-ered the account of his uncontrollable rage in the face of what he perceived to be the desecration of the Temple in Jerusalem, a rage so great that it caused him to overturn the money changers' tables and to whip the money changers themselves. I saw with new eyes the despairing Jesus who sweat blood in the garden and called out to God to "take this cup" from him on the night of his betrayal, the man who cried in anguish from the cross, "My God, my God, why have you forsaken me?" I began to see a Jesus who was more like me, a Jesus I could more easily relate to. The Jesus I found was fully human, even while still somehow fully divine.

My growing awareness of Jesus the person was intertwined with my involvement in what came to be called the "clown ministry" movement of the late 1970s and early 1980s. For years I traveled from church to church, an itinerant preacher, sharing a vision of Jesus quite different from the one on which I'd been raised: a Jesus whose hair was matted, whose robe was stained, and who preached from a boat. We clown ministers emphasized the humanity of Jesus, rather than focusing on his divinity. A Methodist colleague talked about Jesus as a "hunk," reasoning that he must have had pretty well-developed muscles to wield the carpenter's tools of his day. A Catholic priest friend offered the radical image of Jesus laughing and playing with children. (After all, didn't he rebuke his dis-ciples and say, "Suffer the children to come to me?") We preached Jesus the Jester, Jesus the Child, Jesus the Holy Fool.

Yet even as I embraced this ever more human Jesus, my con-ditioning hung around to haunt me. The more human Jesus became, the less divine he seemed, making the foundations of Christianity seem less solid. I talked a good game, but fundamentally I was unable to free myself from the older images. I was trapped in what seemed an insoluble dilemma—either Jesus is the Christ as preached by the church and worthy of my devotion and worship, or he is just a man, and I must go my own way. Eventually, as happened with so many in our culture, I broke with the tradition of my youth and declared that I was no longer a Christian. It seemed that this tradition, this man, had nothing to teach me, and I went searching on other paths.

And yet . . . .

I have never been entirely free of this figure from my past. The religious tradition in which I was raised still has power for me. The images, stories, and lessons of my youth continue to echo in my mind and in my heart. In recent years I have become increasingly aware of something missing—a deep and true connection to life, a sense of wonder that I once took for granted. The more I have drifted from my Christian roots and the further I have gotten away from my "old friend," the more I seem to have lost the connection and wonder that were once a part of my life. Recently I have become increasingly willing to search among those roots to find what I have lost.

I set out to find out whether there is an option between accepting what I now see as unacceptable—the image of Jesus taught to me as a child—and the only other choice I'd ever known—to reject the whole thing. Is there still another Jesus, one who won't strain my credulity yet who can still command my respect and devotion?

This book grew out of my own search in the religious soil that nourished me. In some ways it is a very personal book, reflecting the journey I have taken over the past several years to reacquaint myself with the figure of Jesus Christ, whom I once described in an Easter sermon as "an old friend I seem intent on forgetting."

Yet it is intended not just as a record of my journey but, more importantly, as a guide for your own.

There is a story told in the Gospel of Mark:

> And Jesus went on with his disciples, to the villages of Caesarea Philippi; and on the way he asked his disciples, "Who do the people say that I am?" And they told him, "John the Baptist; and others say, Elijah; and others, one of the prophets." And he asked them, "But who do you say that I am?" (Mark 8:27–29)

While it is interesting to know what others think and have thought about this man, the question that is ultimately important is what *you* say about him. Who do *you* say that he is? Can *you* believe in Jesus? Should you? This book aims to help you answer these questions.

I begin with a look at the secular world in which we live, the world that makes it difficult to discern whether believing in Jesus makes any kind of sense. Picking up the structure of the passage from Mark, in "Modern Views" we turn, as did the disciples, to what others have had to say about this man Jesus. We explore the work of some of those who have been trying to rediscover the Jesus of history, the man behind the myth. If Christianity is about "taking seriously what Jesus took seriously," as theologian and Jesus scholar Marcus Borg suggests, then knowing something about the authentic, historical figure—the carpenter's son who lived some two thousand years ago, the man upon whose life the traditions have been built—would seem an important first step in making a true acquaintance.

In light of this "new" information, we re-examine the Gospel accounts of Jesus' life in "Ancient Visions." Many scholars would agree that the Gospels tell us more about the faith of the early Christians than they do about the historic man from Nazareth, yet the Jesus of tradition is no less "real" than the man who lived in Galilee. The Christ known to the early church, in whom and through whom they understood the man named Jesus, must be engaged as well if this search is to have any meaning beyond mere academic interest. In this section we follow the suggestion of the team of scholars known as the Jesus Seminar and include the Gospel of Thomas along with the more traditional Gospels of Matthew, Mark, Luke, and John.

Next, in "One Answer," we'll face firsthand the challenge of the Gospel story, which states that, after listening to his companions' reports of what others said about who he was, Jesus asked them the more pointed question, "But who do *you* say that I am?" This is truly the only question worth asking when it comes to this powerful, enigmatic figure. Jesus seems not to have been as interested in ideas and ideologies as he was in relationships, and so the question is always personal—Who do *you* say that I am? This chapter presents one possible answer.

Yet for you the reader, this still represents only someone else's response. In this book you'll find some suggestions for how you might find your own answer. I know from my own experience that it is more comfortable to simply read about what others have said and to digest the ideas and experiences others have had, than it is to become personally involved in one's own search. Yet to avoid the personal dimension raised by the question—can *I* believe in Jesus?—is to entirely miss its point. Ultimately, who Jesus was— or is—matters only to the extent that you find the answer to who he was—or is—to *you*.

In the introduction to his book on Jesus, *This Hebrew Lord*, Bishop John Shelby Spong wrote,

> In [the story of Jesus] I found . . . a center for my being. Behind the supernatural framework of the first century . . . I discovered a life I wanted to know; a life that possessed a power I wanted to possess; a freedom, a wholeness for which I had yearned for years."

Many in our world today are seeking such a center, such power, freedom, and wholeness. But why look to Jesus? In one sense, the best answer is another question: Why not? The choice is ours, of course, but why not choose Jesus and his path? What holds us back? What are we afraid of—Jesus, or the choice itself?

At the dramatic height of the story of the Transfiguration, told in both Matthew and Luke, the disciples see a vision of Jesus in conversation with Moses and Elijah, and they hear a voice from heaven saying, "This is my Son, my Beloved; listen to him!"

Note that the voice does not say, "Bow down and worship him," but simply, "Listen to him." How like Marcus Borg's definition of being a Christian: "taking seriously what Jesus took seriously." Perhaps we should take that advice and listen to him. Perhaps this young man, this Jewish peasant from so long ago, deserves another hearing. Perhaps there is more to his message than we were taught in Sunday School. Perhaps this itinerant healer, and teacher, and prophet—whose life and ministry was so short yet whose influence is still felt two thousand years after his death—has something to say to us. And perhaps, if we listen closely—if we have ears to hear—we, too, will find in him what countless others have found and what we have been looking for.

What do we have to lose?

The Secular World

As I began my career as a theologian, the church of which I was a part was risking irrelevancy—or so the rapid decline in participation and membership in mainline and Protestant churches would suggest. Some have said that this was because these churches had ceased to believe anything. I think it was because these churches had ceased to believe anything important. Something important was missing: the very real, historical person by whom the earliest Christians had initially been moved to faith, Jesus of Nazareth, the historical Jesus.

—Steven J. Patterson, *The God of Jesus*

AT ITS INCEPTION, and through much of its history, mainstream America thought of itself as a Christian nation. Some Christians still like to think that their religion is predominant, yet today more Muslims than Episcopalians live in the United States, and it is just as likely that your next door neighbor is a practicing Jew, Sikh, Buddhist, Hindu, Wiccan, or self-proclaimed "eclectic" as it is that she or he belongs to a Christian church. The "Christian nation" was always a myth, of course. But today it is more obviously so. The truth is, we are a multifaith society, as pluralistic religiously as we are in so many other ways.

And we are a society of seekers. People increasingly describe themselves as "spiritual," rather than "religious," apparently believing the words *spirituality* and *religion* to be not only distinct but mutually exclusive. People go to church seeking community, or because they feel they "should." When it comes to feeding their souls, though, many Americans go to retreat centers, into the woods, or almost anywhere but to the churches and synagogues in which they were raised. While public polls report more people saying they attend church today than did ten years ago, mainstream churches report a *decline* in attendance. Somewhat ironically, however, many people who do come back to some form of organized religion after having rejected it in college do so to expose their children to religious instruction—the same instruction, oftentimes, that they spent years rejecting and that they no longer believe themselves!

And even for those who do attend church, things are changing. According to a survey reported in *Newsweek* (March 29, 1999), 93 percent of Christians believe that the man known as Jesus of Nazareth actually lived, and 88 percent believe he rose from the dead. These figures also suggest, however, that 12 percent of the people who consider themselves to be Christians do not believe the stories of the resurrection and that 7 percent believe Jesus *himself* to be fictional! "Christianity" is not the mindless monolith some people assume.

Although these changes may be interesting sociologically, the real issue is the effect they are having on people. Human beings have always sought answers to life's "big questions"—Why am I here? What is the meaning of life? What is the meaning of *my* life? What happens after death? Why be good? How do I know what choices to make? What is important? Religions can be understood as our attempts to express the varied answers we humans have articulated to these questions; they serve as reflections of the various paths we have used to find them. For many today, however, the answers articulated in the past no longer seem meaningful, and the paths themselves seem irrelevant.

This is important, because finding the answers to life's big questions is not easy, and attempting to do so without models or guides makes it that much more difficult. This increased difficulty is evident all around us, as people strive to find meaning in their lives with no clear sense of where to turn for help. The retired Episcopal Bishop of New Jersey, Rev. John Shelby Spong, addresses much of his written work to such people—whom he calls "believers in exile"—about whom he writes:

> We are not able to endure the mental lobotomy that one suspects is the fate of those who project themselves as the unquestioning religious citizens of our age. We do not want to be among those who fear that if we think about what we say about God, either our minds will close down or our faith will explode. We are not drawn to those increasingly defensive religious answers of our generation. Nor are we willing to pretend that these ancient words still have power and meaning for us if they do not. We wonder if it is still possible to be a believer and a citizen of our century at the same time.

Many today answer this question with a resounding, "No!" They turn for their spiritual sustenance to Sufi poetry, Buddhist sutras, Wiccan chants, or the mysteries of chaos theory rather than to the Bible, as if Christianity were irredeemable and all other religious traditions were pure. They are willing—even eager—to listen to the teachings of Tibetan lamas, Hindu avatars, and Mexican shaman, yet hesitant—even resistant—to open themselves to the wisdom of the prophets or the Gospels. When it comes to Christianity, many of us have not only thrown out the baby with the bathwater, but also have tossed out the tub, shut off the lights, and walked out of the house, locking the door behind us.

Yet, to reject an entire religious tradition seems foolhardy, especially when it has so powerfully shaped the development of our culture and, for many of us, our lives. We should be able to cut through the dross of Christianity to find the gold. Over 150 years ago a Unitarian minister, Rev. Theodore Parker, delivered a sermon entitled "The Transient and Permanent in Christianity," in which he wrestled with this same issue:

> Now the solar system as it exists in fact is permanent, though the notions of Thales and Ptolemy, of Copernicus and Descartes about this system, prove transient, imperfect approximations to the true expression. So the Christianity of Jesus is permanent, though what passes for Christianity with Popes and catechisms, with sects and churches, in the first century or in the nineteenth century, prove transient also. . . . Let the Transient pass, fleet as it will . . . God send us a real religious life . . . .

For many today, discerning the "transient" from the "permanent" will require a re-evaluation of the religious tradition in which we were raised, a re-evaluation that will border on a rediscovery. To do so will mean letting go of past associations so that we can see for ourselves what there is to see. For many, this will not be easy. Old patterns are often deeply etched, and it may take an act of great will to see past these relics for something new.

So why bother with this effort? Why try to redeem Jesus and the Christian tradition? Why not simply seek new sources from which to feed our spiritual hunger? A Japanese Buddhist once asked an American aspirant why he was so interested in her religion. "You come from America," she said. "Your roots are in Christianity." She referred to the principles of macrobiotics—eating what is native to your environment rather than artificially adopting a foreign diet—and suggested a religious parallel: If your roots are in Christianity, develop your understanding of that tradition; don't seek your religious nourishment from distant lands.

This is good advice. Something about this man, something about his message, has called to people for over two millennia; something about him may have called to you once. It might be worth looking with your own eyes—and heart, and mind—to see what might be there.

So let's begin with the basics. If Jesus was a real human being who lived in Palestine some two thousand years ago, and if, as most scholars agree, the Christian New Testament is not a journalistic reporting of his life and deeds, then those who want to seek out a fresh understanding of Jesus must first strive to find out what *can* be known about the historical figure. What, if anything, can we know about the man who was, in his own language, Yeshua ben Miriam, Jesus son of Mary?

Modern Views

The historical Jesus is of interest for many reasons. . . . Within a few decades of his death, stories were told about his miraculous birth. By the end of the first century, he was extolled with the most exalted titles known within the religious tradition out of which he came. . . . Within a few centuries he had become Lord of the empire which had crucified him. . . . Thus, simply as a matter of intellectual or historical curiosity, it is interesting to ask, "What was [he] like as a historical person before his death?"

—Marcus J. Borg, *Jesus: A New Vision*

MANY HAVE SAID that the quest for the historical Jesus is a fool's errand, that an attempt to reconstruct the life of a man who lived in first-century Galilee is futile at best and, at worst, misguided. Some argue that the Gospel stories are pure myth and legend, without a trace of history. The "Jesus" we meet in the Christian Bible, they would say, is best thought of as a narrative device. Some would even declare him a fictional construct used by the writers of the Gospels to tell the story of salvation that they understood to be the core of their religion. From such a perspective

7

it would be just as fruitful to look at the legends of Camelot to learn about the historic Celtic king named Arthur, or to watch Errol Flynn to discover the "real" Robin of Locksley. Even the apostle Paul seems to suggest that it is not important to know the Jesus of history. In his Epistle to the Galatians he wrote, "I want you to know, brothers and sisters, that the Gospel that was proclaimed by me is not of human origin; for I did not receive it from a human source, nor was I taught it, but I received it through a revelation of Jesus Christ." Most scholars agree that this and other similar statements are intended to convey that Paul never met the "Jesus of history," that he knew only the "Christ of faith." Apparently, for Paul, that was not a problem.

Others who find the quest for the historical Jesus quixotic do not go so far as to say that the Gospels are "mere myth," but they maintain that it would be nearly impossible to tease out any reliable history from them. Why? For one thing, the Gospels weren't written down until about 60 C.E. Before this, they existed only in oral form. And the oldest surviving copies of these manuscripts date to nearly 175 years after Jesus' death. In *The Five Gospels*, Robert Funk puts the importance of these dates into perspective: Imagine that the Declaration of Independence had originally not been written down but instead was passed on within an oral tradition until the early 1800s when it was finally committed to paper. This document, then, was transcribed and translated, various editors making both "corrections" and mistakes. Imagine, finally, that the earliest surviving copy we have was written in the 1950s. How confident would you feel in its accuracy?

If that weren't enough to make the Gospels suspect as a source of reliable historic information, we must reckon with the fact that we have not one Gospel story, but at least four—each one presenting a different picture of Jesus. Which is the "real" Jesus— the self-aware Cosmic Christ described in the Gospel of John, or the humble healer in that of Mark? Each Gospel writer told the story in a way that made sense to him (or her) and to the audience for which they wrote; they each put their own "spin" on the tale, adding and adapting as needed, telling the story they felt needed to be told. Stephen J. Patterson makes the point in *The God of Jesus* that writers in the ancient world do not seem to have had the same sense of historicity that we do, that there was nothing like our modern journalistic sensibility. How, then, are we to find history in books that were not written to convey history?

Even with these difficulties, many have tried to do just that. While Thomas Jefferson was in the White House, he began the project of cutting his Bible apart and pasting into a notebook the pieces that, to him, made sense. In this way he hoped to discover the "real" Jesus. He wrote of this exercise:

> Among the sayings and discourses imputed to him by his biographers, I find many passages of fine imagination, correct morality, and of the most lovely benevolence; and others again of so much ignorance, so much absurdity, so much untruth, charlatanism, and imposture, as to pronounce it impossible that such contradictions should have proceeded from the same being. I separate therefore the gold from the dross; restore to him the former and leave the latter to the stupidity of some and, roguery of others of his disciples.

The beginning of the intellectual movement known as "the quest for the historical Jesus" is usually dated to the late 1700s and the posthumous publication of the work of Hermann Samuel Reimarus. Reimarus was a German scholar who suggested that a distinction could—and should—be made between what Jesus said about himself and what the Gospel writers said about him. This led to a distinction between what is commonly called "the Jesus of history" and "the Christ of faith," the former coming from Jesus' own words about himself and the latter being the assertions about him from the early Christian community.

This first phase of the quest for the historical Jesus lasted through the early 1800s and generated hundreds of books and articles focused on the human Jesus, the Jesus of history. Many of these works attempted to find rational explanations for the more unbelievable aspects of the Gospel stories—the reported miracles—striving to bridge the growing gap between the traditional stories and the more modern, more scientific understandings of how the world works. These early searchers wanted to uncover the man behind the myths. Their guiding assumption was that the authors of the Gospels wanted to report about the life of the man from Galilee but were not particularly accurate reporters—being of a "simpler age," the Gospel writers were too quick to see magic and miracle, and so distorted the record they intended to leave for future generations.

In the late nineteenth and early twentieth centuries, the quest for the historical Jesus was largely discontinued because of the prevalent perception of the time that the Gospels could not be seen as a source of any useful historical information at all, that they are essentially mythic tales woven to express the central religious ideas of their authors. It was also argued that even if we could get good history from the Gospels, knowing the Jesus of history is relatively unimportant; what matters is knowing the Christ of faith. In other words, the living presence of Jesus encountered in tradition and in the lives of the faithful was understood as far more important than the historic person upon whom the faith traditions were built. From this perspective, to seek the Jesus of history is to take the wrong track; one should seek to encounter the living Christ of faith instead.

These two views—that the Bible stories are mythic tales with no underlying historicity, and that such historical grounding would be unimportant at any rate—influenced Christian thinkers throughout most of the twentieth century. In the early 1950s, however, theologians began to ask again how it could be possible that the Jesus of history could be seen as unimportant to the religious tradition built on his name. In fact, they argued, that history should be seen as fundamentally important, since Christianity makes the claim that God acts in history; the center of Christian teaching is not just that God was incarnate in *some* person but that God was incarnate in *this particular* person. Who this person was, then, would seem to be worth discovering.

This second wave of searching lasted about a decade before fading, as intellectual movements often do. The quest for the historical Jesus was revived most recently in 1985 when a group of biblical scholars—coming from a variety of religious backgrounds—formed the Jesus Seminar and brought the quest for the historical Jesus out of the halls of academia and into the public eye. Academics and seminary-trained ministers have long taken much of this historical work for granted, yet it has not often been shared with the people in their congregations. This is changing, and the quest for the historical Jesus is now much more widely based. John Shelby Spong, in *Why Christianity Must Change or Die*, notes that this shift is absolutely necessary if Christianity is to have any hope of surviving.

Spong's sense of urgency was voiced over one hundred years earlier by Ralph Waldo Emerson when he wrote,

> Christ preached the greatness of mankind, but we hear only the greatness of Christ. . . . Is it not time to present this matter of Christianity exactly as it is, to take away all false reverence for Jesus, and not mistake the stream for the source? . . . I cannot but think that Jesus Christ will be better loved by being less adored . . . it was thought to add to the dignity of Christ to make him king, to make him God. Now that the scriptures are read with purged eyes, it is seen that he is only to be loved for so much goodness and wisdom as was in him, which are the only things for which a sound human mind can love any person.

In 1841 Rev. Theodore Parker sounded a similar theme in
"The Transient and Permanent in Christianity": "The Christianity of Jesus is permanent, though what passes for Christianity
with Popes and catechisms, with sects and churches, in the first
century or in the nineteenth century, prove transient also." He
spent the rest of that sermon, and a great deal of his career, trying to distinguish between the transient and the permanent in
his religion. Today, many stress a distinction between "the religion *of* Jesus" and "the religion *about* Jesus" and suggest that we
should move closer to the former and stay away from the latter.
Knowing as much as we can about the actual man, then, would
seem essential.

Yet even if we agree that searching for information about the
historical Jesus is important, the question remains—how do we
do it? How do we address the formidable objections raised by
opponents of the search—the tremendous time gap between the
events being described and the sources we have to study, for example? If we're going to engage this search, we will need to affirm
four basic assumptions before we can begin:

- A man named Jesus (Hebrew, *Yeshua*) lived in the Galilee
  region of Palestine sometime between the years 4 B.C.E. and
  36 C.E.
- A distinction exists between the "Jesus of history" and the
  "Christ of faith."
- The Gospels are rather *un*helpful (although not useless) in
  teaching about the historic Jesus.
- We will never know about the historic Jesus with absolute
  certainty, but we can make well-educated guesses.

Scholars use a rigorous three-step process to produce these
well-educated guesses. The first step is to build a foundational
context through cross-cultural anthropological study—what do
we know about what it was like to live in a pre-industrial, agrar-

ian society? What social structures can we expect to find, for instance? What belief systems? What patterns and practices?

The second step is to examine the environment of the Judeo-Roman world—what do we know about what life was like in this particular pre-industrial agrarian society? What do we know about what was happening during the time of Jesus and while the Gospels were written? What, then, would we expect to be true of someone who lived in that particular time and place?

Finally, we compare these expectations with the Gospel stories. For example, we can know how wandering holy men and healers have been seen in pre-industrial agrarian societies, and there are non-biblical sources that tell us what people expected of Jewish holy men and healers in first-century Palestine. If we then examine the Gospels to see how the early Christian community's memories of Jesus match with these other sources of information, we can begin to draw a picture of the historic person of Jesus. John Dominic Crossan demonstrates the value of this process:

> If, for example, we are tempted to describe Jesus as a literate middle-class carpenter, cross-cultural anthropology reminds us that there was no middle class in ancient societies and that peasants are usually illiterate; so how could Jesus become what never existed at his time?

Even with the best methodology, we will never be able to know with complete certainty what Jesus, the historical person, was really like, yet by building this three-part structure—each part developing and clarifying the one before it—we can make the claim that at least our guesses are well educated. Still, there remains one final hurdle. In *The Quest for the Historical Jesus*, Albert Schweitzer noted that such a quest can be like looking into a deep well and seeing there only one's own reflection. We know so little about the historical Jesus that when we look for him we tend to find what we are looking for. This is why the Jesus Seminar has written,

The final test is to ask whether the Jesus we have found is the Jesus we wanted to find. The last temptation is to create Jesus in our own image, to marshal the facts to support preconceived convictions. This fatal pitfall has prompted the Jesus seminar to adopt as its final general rule of evidence: *beware of finding a Jesus entirely congenial to you.*

If we are careful, if we are wary of finding our own reflection, and if we remind ourselves constantly of the tentative nature of our discoveries, there is still much that we can learn.

And what *do* we learn in such a search? Who is the Jesus we encounter? Certainly not the white European Jesus with the blue eyes and flowing blonde hair. Perhaps the most important—yet frequently overlooked—fact is that Jesus was a Middle Eastern Jew. The major theme in Spong's *This Hebrew Lord* is that in order to have any hope of understanding the historical Jesus, we need to remind ourselves that he was born to Jewish parents and raised in a Jewish culture. He was, by all accounts, steeped in the scriptures of Judaism, and he practiced the faith of his people. His early followers were, for the most part, other Jews, and it is clear that at least his earliest understanding of his mission was as a spiritual renewal of Judaism. To connect with the Jesus who lived and breathed, we have to dig back through what Spong calls the "Grecianization" of the Gospel to find its Hebrew roots. We have to cut through the overlay of Greek philosophy that informed the writers of the Gospels—and threatens to bury the Jewish man.

Jesus was involved in a movement to revitalize Judaism. It seems quite clear that he did not set out to create a new religion but rather to renew and reform the tradition in which he had been born. He is quoted in the Gospel of Matthew as saying, "Do not think that I have come to abolish the law or the prophets; I have come not to abolish but to fulfill."

Whether Jesus understood himself to be the Messiah, an embodiment of Second Isaiah's "Suffering Servant," a prophet, or a
man in whom and through whom God was working, it seems clear
that he did not see himself as the founder of a new religion. The
historical Jesus wanted to bring about a renewal in Judaism; he
wanted to bring his people closer to their God. Jesus sought to
shift the emphasis back from God's holiness to God's compassion.
Rather than stress that we should become "holy as God is holy,"
Jesus' message to his fellow Jews was that they should be "compassionate as God is compassionate." Compassion is central to the
teaching of Jesus. This seems indisputable, even though the Gospel writers often put conflicting messages into his mouth.

What else can we know or deduce about the historical Jesus?
We know that Jesus lived about one hundred years after Rome
had spread the *Pax Romana* into his homeland. During this time,
most of the people in the Roman Empire—some 80 percent of the
population—lived at a subsistence level. The Roman social sys-
tem was shaped like a pyramid, with the emperor on top, supported by retainers who were supported by merchants, traders, and
others, who were in turn supported by the work of the vast majority of the people. This lowest stratum of the population made the
Pax Romana possible, but at tremendous cost. As Stephen Patterson
put it in *The God of Jesus*, "Rome slowly siphoned the life out of
places like Palestine."

There were more immediate and brutal costs, as well. Shortly
before Jesus' birth, the Roman General Varus quelled a peasant uprising in Palestine by attacking the cities of Galilee and Samaria, selling
their inhabitants into slavery and publicly crucifying two thousand
of the uprising's leaders. Shortly after Jesus' death, all the people of
the nearby towns of Gophna, Emmaus, Lydda, and Thamma were
sold into slavery because they had been slow to pay their share of the
Judean tribute to Rome. This was the world in which Jesus lived, and
we can be sure that this environment affected him.

We can be sure, too, that within the birth stories of Jesus there is at least a nugget of truth, although as they come down to us they are clearly the stuff of myth. Almost certainly, for instance, Jesus was poor. You would expect his chroniclers to have invented an auspicious birth, a birth that marked him from his beginnings as a person of power, worthy of respect. They tried—there are all those angels, and magi, and gifts of gold and myrrh—but the Gospel writers apparently had no way of getting around the fact that Jesus was born to poor parents. He was not a Siddhartha Guatama, overcoming the "obstacle" of inherent power and prestige to become the enlightened Buddha. Jesus of Nazareth knew poverty and oppression; he understood suffering from firsthand experience.

The story of Jesus' parentage also seems to contain some truth. It is remembered that when Jesus returns to preach in Nazareth his neighbors call out, "is this not . . . the son of Mary?" This was a description that was used when one's patrilineage was unknown. If Joseph had been Jesus' father, Jesus would have been called "son of Joseph"; that he was called "son of Mary" strongly suggests that the identity of Jesus' father was at least in question. In fact, in disputes between Jews and early Christians, the charge was frequently made that Jesus was the "illegitimate" child of Mary and a Roman soldier.

The author of the Gospel of Mark makes no mention at all of Jesus' birth, but both Luke and Matthew go to great lengths to explain how and why Joseph was not Jesus' real father, that Jesus was literally the son of God. That they go to such lengths, rather than just gloss over such details, implies that they were being forced to deal with known, and irrefutable, facts. Stephen Mitchell, in *The Gospel According to Jesus*, makes much of this point and explores it at length, suggesting that this legacy of "illegitimacy" might explain Jesus' passionate relationship with God as his "father."

Whatever its origins, we can also be sure that an intimate, personal relationship with God was part of the make-up of the historical Jesus. He lived in a time when people believed in a spiritual dimension, a world of Spirit, and it is clear that Jesus was, in Marcus Borg's words, a "Spirit-filled person." That Jesus was Spirit-filled might appear so obvious as to be redundant, yet that quality is such a relatively rare thing in today's world as to be worth mentioning. Jesus was a man who lived his life in communion with the divine—he took time for solitary prayer to feed and deepen his connection, and when he acted, he did so from a place of Spirit. The historical Jesus was a man in whom others saw the face of God. He was so in touch with the sacred that he seemed to be "as one" with it, and when those who knew Jesus looked back on their relationship with him, they could describe it only by calling Jesus "God."

It is also clear that an intimate connection with Spirit flowed through the historical Jesus in acts of healing. All of the Gospel writers agree that Jesus was known as a healer; the few independent sources that make reference to him attest to this as well. Again and again, we read stories of Jesus' healing work, and of crowds coming to him specifically for his ability to heal. He not only felt connected to Spirit—Spirit flowed through him. He was not unique in this; history tells us that many people in Jesus' day were known for their ability to heal, as there are people with this gift today.

Yet, to see the historical Jesus as a purely "spiritual" person with no connection to the "real" world would be a mistake. Such a split would have been unthinkable to a first-century Jewish mind; no world existed apart from the world of God. Reread the Psalms and, especially, the prophets to see how closely what we would call the religious and the secular realms were linked in the Hebrew worldview. When Jesus spoke of "the kingdom of God" he was making a religious point but also an explicitly "political" reference. The Greek word that is usually translated as "kingdom" is *basileia*, which in just about every other ancient text is translated as "empire." In Jesus' day there was only one empire—the empire of Rome. To speak of an empire *of God* was to guarantee comparison with the empire of Rome, a comparison that would not have been flattering to the Romans. Thus, even Jesus' religious message carried political overtones. Considering the political environment in which Jesus lived, John Dominic Crossan believes that one of the few facts of Jesus' life we can be sure of is that he was executed by Rome as a political criminal.

The picture that emerges of the historical Jesus is of a young man who knew firsthand the weight of oppression and what it was to be downcast and crushed, yet who also knew firsthand a deep and unshakable connection to that creative, dynamic spirit called God. He knew himself to be in relationship with God and felt himself called to be not only a voice but also an embodiment of that holy reality that he saw so clearly. Others saw it too. In the words and deeds of this itinerant preacher, teacher, and healer, others were able to see God as if face-to-face. He sought a renewal of the religion of his day, yet ultimately the political dimensions of his vision were seen as a threat by the Roman establishment and he was put to death. This is what we can know of the Jesus of history.

As we seek to reacquaint ourselves with this "old friend," recognizing that Jesus was a real man who lived a real life is vitally important. The portrait of the person who emerges from the quest for the historical figure is deeply moving: a young, passionate, "God-intoxicated" person who believed so deeply in his principles and ideals that he was willing to suffer and die for them. It also seems undeniable that the vision and, in some senses, the life of this remarkable man did not end with his death. Those who had been with him felt an ongoing presence that they understood to be his; they continued his work in his name. We turn, now, to their stories to continue our search.

Ancient Visions

No man's life can be encompassed in one telling. There is no
way to give each year its allotted weight, to include each event,
each person who helped to shape a lifetime. What can be done
is to be faithful in spirit to the record and try to find one's way
to the heart of the man.

—Richard Attenborough, *Gandhi*

THE GOSPELS should be considered with two caveats.

The first, which we discussed earlier, is that none of them is a
firsthand account of the life and times of *Yeshua ben Miriam*. The
texts—the earliest of which was written over a generation after
Jesus died—evolved over centuries of amendments, embellish-
ments, and appendices. The Gospels are not eyewitness journalism, whatever else they may be.

In 1993, the Jesus Seminar published the results of their more
than ten-year study aimed at discerning which of the words ascribed to Jesus were actually spoken by the man and which were
written by others and put into his mouth. These scholars, from a
variety of traditions, developed a set of guidelines to help them
determine the authenticity of the 1,500 or so sayings attributed to

Jesus. These guidelines included asking such questions as whether the saying was already well known in Jesus' day and whether it too conveniently supports a doctrinal position of the early church. Do two or more of the authors record the saying or is there only one reference? Does the saying "sound" like Jesus or does it fit more with the style, tone, and agenda of the Gospel's author? Many of the seminar's criteria are based on well-established principles of historical and literary scholarship; others are undeniably subjective. Taken as a whole, though, they provide the seminar members with a clear standard by which to make their determinations.

After considering each of the sayings against these "rules of evidence," the scholars voted with colored beads: red for sayings they felt sure originated with Jesus; pink for sayings that they were unsure of yet which they were inclined to include; gray for sayings about which they were doubtful; and black for those sayings that they felt fairly certain were not original. When the votes were averaged, fully 82 percent of the sayings recorded in the scriptures and revered by tradition as being spoken by Jesus were considered to be doubtful at best. Again, the Gospels are not journalism.

The second caveat to a consideration of the Gospels is the reminder that the Gospels of Matthew, Mark, Luke, and John are, in fact, only the four that were declared authoritative in the fourth century and are recognized as part of the New Testament today. The earliest Christians made a great many other attempts—including such texts as the Gospel of the Egyptian, the Gospel of Phillip, and the Gospel of Mary—to tell the story of Jesus, to make sense of this powerful figure's life. During the first centuries of the Christian church, various communities came to different understandings as to which scriptures were to be considered sacred, and a number of different collections are known to have been used—at one time or another, by one group or another, all were considered authoritative. The first reference to the New Testament in the form we know it today—the four Gospels, the Book of Acts, the twenty-one Epistles, and the Book of Revelation—is in a letter written by Bishop Athanasius of Alexandria, in 367 C.E. Until that time, each of what we now call the apocryphal books had enjoyed a claim to authenticity equal to those we think of as scripture today.

Much can be learned from a reading of these other Gospels. They tell stories that are recorded nowhere else—Jesus' first miracle, apparently, was not turning water into wine at the wedding in Cana, as the Gospel of John records it. According to one of these apocryphal Gospels, when Jesus was an infant his mother threw her baby's bathwater out of the window and it landed on a passing leper, instantly curing him; and when Jesus was a toddler, he would form clay doves that he then brought to life. More important than such stories, however, these apocryphal Gospels remind us that the early Christian community explored a number of ways of understanding the life and ministry of the man named Jesus. What we think of as Christianity today is but one of many possible expressions.

In this chapter, however, we will limit our search for Jesus to the stories of recognized tradition—the four familiar Gospels of Matthew, Mark, Luke, and John—with one addition, the Gospel of Thomas. This Gospel is an example of what is called a "sayings" Gospel, a list of sayings without any connecting narrative structure. Many scholars believe that a text such as this was used by the authors of Matthew and Luke in the preparation of their own Gospels. This is the so-called Q hypothesis—so named from the German Quelle, or "source." For centuries there was no direct evidence of such a sayings Gospel, yet it was assumed that Q existed because Matthew and Luke have so much material in common, found nowhere else, that it made sense to posit a common source. The discovery of the Gospel of Thomas in 1945 gave support to the Q hypothesis by proving that such sayings Gospels did exist. For this reason, we will include it in our considerations.

Scholars generally agree that Mark was written between 65 and 70 C.E., Matthew between 80 and 85 C.E., Luke between 85 and 90 C.E., and John somewhere around 100 C.E. This chronology is not unequivocally certain—some believe that John was written first, rather than last, for instance. Most, however, agree that among the canonical scriptures Mark was written first and that the authors of both Matthew and Luke were familiar with and drew upon his work. This would account for the tremendous similarity among these three Gospels, a similarity so striking that they are known as the *synoptic Gospels*—that is, they can be "seen together."

Those who hold to this theory see John as an independent tradition. Many differences set John and the synoptics apart. Only in John, for instance, is Jesus described as a self-aware "Cosmic Christ," in whom and through whom the world is made. John tells stories that are in none of the other Gospels and leaves out events that the others all report. Jesus' ministry could be as short as one year from baptism until crucifixion, according to the synoptics; in John it is at least three years long.

Yet, despite the differences among the Gospels, in many people's minds the four are seen as one. Matthew's and Luke's birth accounts, for instance, merge as if there is only one story. Even though only Matthew talks about magi and only Luke mentions the shepherds—and Mark and John say nothing about Jesus' birth at all!—we usually think that "the Gospels" tell one story with all of the details included. It is true that, taken together, the four Gospels create a single portrait of "the Christ of faith" upon whom the traditional teachings of the Christian church have been based, yet each of these books presents its own unique picture of the man Jesus. It is important, if we are to learn as much as possible about the man we seek, that we try to learn what we can from each of the different portraits.

The Gospel of Mark

Ancient tradition ascribes the authorship of the Gospel of Mark to the disciple John Mark, who is mentioned in the Book of Acts. It is said that he wrote it while in Rome, as a summary of the Apostle Peter's teaching. Although nearly universally accepted evidence shows it to be the first written, Mark is placed second in the New Testament. It is the shortest of the Gospels—the whole of Mark comprises only sixteen chapters compared with John's twenty-one, Luke's twenty-four, and Matthew's twenty-eight. Reading Mark, one is surprised at what is *not* included—the miraculous birth, for instance. Jesus' birth isn't mentioned at all. Mark begins his story with John the Baptist preaching repentance and baptizing in the wilderness. Jesus' first appearance is when he, already a young man, goes to John for baptism and hears God's affirmation, "You are my Son, the Beloved; with you I am well pleased."

Also missing from Mark is any account of post-resurrection appearances by Jesus. Some ancient manuscripts included such stories, and most Bibles today incorporate them even though the majority of scholars agree that Mark originally ended on a more ambiguous note: having returned to the tomb after the Sabbath to anoint Jesus' body, Mary Magdalene, Mary (the mother of James), and Salome discover the tomb to be empty except for "a young man, dressed in a white robe" who tells them that Jesus has been raised and that they should go and tell the disciples that "he is going ahead of you to Galilee." The generally agreed-upon last line of the original text is, "So they went out and fled from the tomb, for terror and amazement had seized them; and they said nothing to anyone, for they were afraid."

So what *is* in the book of Mark? A lot of action. Although Mark's Jesus says he came to preach, we read mostly about the things he did, rather than the things he said. Fewer words are attributed to Jesus in this Gospel than in any of the others. Mark's

Jesus is a man of action, and the Gospel is written in an active style; the Greek word that translates as "immediately" or "at once" is used no fewer than forty times in this relatively short book.

Mark's Jesus is a healer—there are sixteen specific references to healing. Wherever Jesus went, we are told, crowds gathered of people who sought his healing power. Mark's Jesus is also a man with a secret. Nearly every "unclean spirit" he encounters recognizes him as the "Holy One of God," or "Son of the Most High God." Even his own disciples proclaim him to be "Messiah" and see him radiantly transfigured and standing alongside Moses and Elijah—yet in every case he warns them to say nothing to anyone about it. This is what New Testament scholars refer to as "the messianic secret," one of Mark's distinguishing features.

Jesus' teaching, too, seems to be something of a secret. He tells his disciples that he teaches with parables so that the masses who hear him "may indeed look, but not perceive, and may indeed listen, but not understand." He promises to explain himself to his disciples in secret so that they, at least, may understand the truth of his teachings; yet even after doing so, they still do not understand.

At one point, in apparent frustration, Jesus says to them, "Do you still not see or understand? Are your hearts hardened? Do you have eyes, and fail to see? Do you have ears, and fail to hear? And do you not remember?" He is referring specifically to the two miraculous feedings Mark records, one of which they have just experienced together. In each of these instances Jesus had instructed his disciples to feed the crowds who had been following them, even though there was far too little food with which to do so. In one case they had five loaves of bread and two fish, and in the other they had seven loaves and "a few" fish, yet the crowds numbered in the thousands. But despite their apparent lack in the face of obviously overwhelming need, the disciples are able to feed everyone. They even manage to collect several baskets of leftovers.

Later, Jesus, reminding his disciples of these incidents, marvels that his companions have not understood what they've experienced. Yet he offers his friends no real clue as to the meaning
of these events. Were the feedings to be understood in comparison to the story from the Hebrew scriptures in which the prophet
Elisha fed a group of one hundred with only twenty loaves of
bread? Were they to be understood as both literal and symbolic
manifestations of God's bounty? Were they to be signs of encouragement in the face of life's challenges? Despite his amazement that the disciples have not understood, Jesus gives them
no definitive explanation.

The Jesus of Mark is an enigmatic man—a preacher who is
better remembered for his deeds than his words; a teacher who
intentionally speaks in riddles and whose closest students do not
understand him; a man whom the "unclean" recognize and the
"righteous" reject; and a Messiah who strives to keep his true identity a secret.

The Gospel of Matthew

Tradition holds that the Gospel of Matthew was written by the
disciple Matthew, a tax collector who was also known as "Levi."
This attribution dates back to the writings of Irenaeus, in the second century, yet there is little evidence to support it. Rather than
being an original, firsthand account—as it would have been if
one of Jesus' disciples had written it—most scholars agree that
the anonymous author of the Gospel of Matthew was familiar with,
and made liberal use of, Mark's Gospel as he told his own version
of the story of Jesus of Nazareth. It is no mere copy, however.
While Matthew incorporates many stories and sayings that are in
Mark, they are not always in the same order, nor are they always
told with the same intent. Also, there is much in Matthew that is
not to be found in Mark at all.

Matthew begins his story with Jesus' genealogy in order to prove Jesus' royal descent. He traces Jesus' lineage back through King David all the way to Abraham himself; this is no ordinary Jewish peasant! Even Jesus' birth, as told by Matthew, elevates him above the norm—he is said to be the son of no less than the Holy Spirit, and his miraculous conception is understood as the fulfillment of prophecy. Right away, we see one of Matthew's chief concerns: to establish Jesus' "credentials" as messiah, to demonstrate that the life of Jesus was the fulfillment of Jewish prophecy and expectation. While all of the Gospel writers describe Jesus as fulfilling scriptural prophecy, none does so more emphatically than Matthew—he includes nine "proof-texts" that are in none of the other Gospels. He also refers more often to Jesus' Davidic lineage, reporting six testimonials to the idea that Jesus is a descendent of the house of King David that appear in no other Gospel. New Testament scholars have inferred from the author's apparent agenda that he was writing for the Jewish–Christian communities in Syria or Palestine and so took great pains to portray Jesus as the answer to Jewish prayers for a messiah.

Matthew describes Jesus as the new Moses, drawing a number of parallels between the stories he tells of Jesus and the stories his audience would have known about Moses:

- Herod's slaughter of the children after Jesus' birth parallels Pharaoh's similar massacre.
- Jesus grew up in Egypt and then returned to Israel, as did Moses.
- Both men spent time in the wilderness (Jesus fasted for forty days and Moses wandered for forty years).
- The wilderness experience of both men was preceded by the crossing of water—the Red Sea for Moses and the Jordan River for Jesus.
- Moses divided the people of Israel into twelve tribes and Jesus chose twelve disciples.

- Moses gave Israel the law of God, and Matthew's Jesus reaffirms and then expands that law in his own teaching.
- It can even be argued that, as Moses led the people of Israel out of their bondage in Egypt, Matthew's Jesus is leading humanity away from their bondage to sin.

The Gospel of Matthew appears to be more of a conscious literary construction than does the Gospel of Mark. Literary devices abound—the parallels with the story of Moses, for example. And Matthew's Gospel simply seems to have more—more storytelling, more teachings, more evidence of Jesus' life as fulfillment of Jewish prophecy and expectation. Even the material Matthew shares with the other synoptic Gospels has been expanded. For instance, where Luke's Jesus meets a blind man on the road, Matthew's Jesus meets two; where Mark and Luke tell of Jesus driving out demons from a single man who lived among the tombs, Matthew's Jesus faces two demoniacs.

The Jesus of Matthew is also much more a man of words than is Mark's. Matthew has organized Jesus' teachings into five major discourses—a parallel, perhaps, to the five books of Moses—filled with insightful and memorable lessons. Reading these speeches, one is struck by both the powerful beauty of the ideas expressed and the feeling that Matthew's Jesus was jumping almost wildly from thought to thought—as if he has so much to say that he tries to say it all at once. If Mark's Jesus is a man of great action, Matthew's is a man of great wisdom. He is also—unlike Mark's humble Jesus—a man who is not shy about claiming his authority.

Yet Matthew's portrait of Jesus also shows us the evolution of Jesus' understanding and teaching in a way the other Gospels do not. Early in his ministry, Jesus chooses twelve disciples and sends them out to teach and heal. He specifically commands them, however, not to enter foreign lands but to focus their attention and energy on "the lost sheep of the house of Israel." By the end of

Matthew, however, the risen Jesus declares that his disciples are to go out to "all the nations."

What could account for the change? About halfway between these two passages, Matthew tells a story—one that is also included in Luke. At first glance it might appear to be just another healing story—a woman comes to Jesus asking him to heal her daughter. In this case, the woman is not Jewish; she's a foreigner, a Syrophoenician (or Canaanite). Jesus repeats his narrow understanding of his mission, "I was not sent except to the lost sheep of the house of Israel." But the woman does not give up. She asks again, and Jesus' answer displays a bigoted cruelty that is surprising in an exalted God-man but which is sadly believable in an all too human person. He says, "It is not good to take the children's bread and throw it to the dogs."

And then Matthew describes a miracle. The woman refuses to be stopped by this humiliating comparison. She tries again— her daughter's life is at stake—"Yes, Lord, yet even the dogs eat the crumbs which fall from their masters' tables." With her answer she stands up for herself, affirms her right to be recognized, and asserts her humanity. And the miracle is not the subsequent healing of her daughter, it is that Jesus never again sees the world through such limited eyes and never again says that his mission is only to the people of his own nation. This story shows Jesus learning from this remarkable woman and the depth of his ministry growing as a result.

The Gospel of Matthew has been called "the church's Gospel," and it certainly presents us with a familiar figure. Yet somehow this Jesus remains ultimately unembraceable. Perhaps he is too familiar, or maybe he feels too much like a literary creation— too reminiscent of the cutout figure from Sunday School.

The Gospel of Luke

Scholars agree that the Gospel of Luke was probably written in Caesarea or, possibly, Rome, somewhere near the end of the first century and was aimed at non-Jewish readers, most likely cultured Romans. It is the first of two books; the author continues the story begun here in the Book of Acts.

The Gospel of Luke has been attributed to Luke, a Gentile convert, a physician, and a friend of the Apostle Paul who is mentioned in several of Paul's Epistles. It begins, "Inasmuch as many have undertaken to compile a narrative of the things which have been accomplished among us . . . it seemed good to me also, having followed all things closely for some time past, to write an orderly account for you . . . that you may know the truth concerning the things of which you have been informed."

The sense that we are getting "an orderly account" is more prevalent in Luke's Gospel than any of the others. This is not to say that Luke does not exalt its main character—its genealogy of Jesus extends past Abraham all the way to Adam! Still, Luke's depiction of Jesus feels more "real," more human, than any other we have seen.

We are given far more humanizing background in Luke, for instance, than in any of the other Gospels. We learn that John the Baptist was Jesus' cousin—not just another powerful religious figure with whom Jesus interacted—he literally was family. We are told the story of John's conception and birth, and about a beautiful reunion between Mary and her kinswoman Elizabeth, John's mother, during their pregnancies. Much more is told in Luke about Jesus' own birth than we read anywhere else, and Luke is the only source for the story from Jesus' childhood about his trip to the temple in Jerusalem at age twelve. As Luke tells it, Jesus' parents set out to return home from a visit to Jerusalem and find that their son is nowhere to be found. Frantically they retrace their steps, ultimately finding him in the temple court, conversing with the elders. When his mother asks him why he did such a thing he responds in such a way that you can hear the twelve-year-old boy in his words, "Why were you looking for me? Didn't you know I had to be in my Father's house?" Stories such as this make Luke's Jesus feel more like a real person than either Matthew's or Mark's.

And Luke is not as interested as Matthew is in demonstrating that Jesus was the fulfillment of Jewish prophecy; so Luke's Jesus seems much more a free moral agent. Luke does not give the reader the feeling that Jesus goes places or does things in order to fulfill what was written in the prophets. Luke's Jesus goes places and does and says things for the same reasons we do today: When someone asks him a question, he answers; when he encounters a situation, he responds. Like the other synoptic writers, Luke demonstrates that many of Jesus' words and deeds did, in fact, fulfill prophecy and expectation; yet, unlike Matthew, he makes it seem more a response than a predicate. Luke's Jesus seems to have a much freer will than Matthew's and in this way, too, he is more believable.

Overall, Luke presents a more balanced portrait of Jesus. Luke's Jesus is not the "driven" man of action we find in Mark, nor the indefatigable teacher we meet in Matthew. A passage indicative of Luke's portrait reads, "When the crowds learned [that he was in Bethsaida], they followed him; and he welcomed them and spoke to them of the kingdom of God, and cured those who had need of healing." Luke's Jesus teaches about God's empire and cures those who need healing; those two things sum up his life and his ministry.

It is only in Luke that we find the story of the two disciples, on the road to Emmaus, talking with Jesus—after his death. The two disciples are walking home, trying to make sense of what they have just experienced watching Jesus' crucifixion, when they are met on the road by a man they do not recognize. He speaks to them in a way that makes the significance of everything that has happened become clear to them—their hearts "burn" within them, and the meaning of the Jewish scriptures is opened to them. They understand everything, "beginning with Moses and all the prophets," for the first time. They invite this stranger to stay and eat with them. As he breaks bread at their table, they recognize their companion as none other than Jesus himself. He promptly vanishes from their sight.

This story about the risen Jesus providing a clear summation of his earthly life and teaching is in keeping with the "orderly account" the author of Luke aimed to write. And, at least in part because of this attempt to tell the whole story, the Jesus of Luke seems more real than any other Jesus encountered in the scriptures thus far; he seems less a crafted character and more of a man.

The Gospel of John

The Gospel of John is said to be written by the disciple John and is so unlike the others that many scholars consider it a separate tradition. John is often referred to as the "spiritual" Gospel, because it deals much more with "spirit" than do the other Gospels, and it portrays Jesus in a much more cosmic way. One need only compare the starting points of the canonical Gospels to understand this distinction. Mark begins with Jesus' baptism; Matthew begins with Jesus' genealogy and conception; Luke begins with the conception of Jesus' cousin, John the Baptist. The Gospel of John begins with the beginning of time itself:

> In the beginning was the Word, and the Word was with God, and the Word was God. He was in the beginning with God; all things were made through him and without him was not anything made that was made. In him was life, and the life was the light of men.

From the outset we are told that this Jesus is no mere man.

Much in John's portrait of Jesus draws people to Christianity; much in John's portrait pushes people away. John's Jesus is more Christ than man; he is depicted as not truly of this world but, rather, a creature from heaven who has come down to fulfill a specific mission. If Matthew's Jesus appears to be a puppet dancing to the needs of prophecy, John's Jesus is the puppeteer, pulling the strings of those around him to accomplish his Father's purpose.

John understands Jesus to be much more central to his own message than do any of the other Gospel writers. It has been said that in the synoptic Gospels the focus of Jesus' teaching is God but that in John his focus is himself. John's Jesus sees himself as the "living water," the "bread of life," and the "light of the world." John's Gospel is, in fact, the only source of the well-known "I am" statements—"I am the vine"; "I am the good shepherd"; and "I am the way, and the truth, and the life." In none of the other canonical Gospels does Jesus speak so directly, nor in such elevated terms, about himself.

Only in John do we find that succinct summary of traditional Christian theology that is so often seen on signs at sporting events, John 3:16—"For God so loved the world that he gave his only Son, that whoever believes in him should not perish but have eternal life." This more elevated and elaborate Christology is one reason that many scholars think John is the latest Gospel. Religious concepts usually get more complicated as time goes on rather than more simple. In other words, enough time had to pass for the early Christians to develop their picture of Jesus from the humble vision of Mark to the Cosmic Christ of John.

There is something in this powerful portrait that is appealing. This is a Jesus who knows who he is and who can speak authoritatively about matters of the spirit because he is, in many ways, more spirit than matter. You can believe it when he declares, "I will not leave you desolate. . . . I am in my Father, and you in me, and I in you." You can feel the strength of his promise, "Truly,

truly, I say to you, he who believes in me will also do the works that I do; and greater works than these will he do. . . ." When he speaks of eternal life, you can take comfort from the obvious fact that he does so from experience. And when he says, "These things I have spoken to you, that my joy may be in you, and that your joy may be full," he inspires an exciting vision indeed.

Yet this Jesus also brings to mind the story of a Zen master. There is a Buddhist sutra that has Siddhartha declare immediately after his birth, "No one before me, no one behind me, I alone am the World Honored One." Reflecting on this scripture the Master declared, "If I had been there and heard him say such a thing I would have cut him into pieces and fed him to the dogs." The kind of grandiloquent statements John's Jesus makes about himself seem out of place coming from the mouth of a truly enlightened being. You would expect a little more humility.

Nonetheless, even though the Gospel of John is outside the synoptic tradition, it is deeply woven into the fabric of Christianity. John's profound differences from the other Gospels are often overlooked because of their assumed unanimity—unless it is pointed out, people rarely notice how different they are. And yet, while John offers us little about the human Jesus, as a poetic meditation on Jesus' effect on the early community John literally stands alone.

The Gospel of Thomas

Reading the Gospel of Thomas is a remarkable experience. It is not a Gospel in the traditional sense; there is no narrative, no plot line, no story. Thomas is simply a collection of 114 sayings attributed to Jesus, most with little more than the introduction, "He said," or, "Jesus said," to set them apart from one another. It is, in some ways, more like the *Tao te Ching* than what one expects from Christian scripture—it is teaching without context or commentary. In this it resembles—and gives credence to the theoreti-

cal existence of—the source material Q, from which both Matthew and Luke hypothetically drew. The discovery of Thomas
proved that such "sayings Gospels" did indeed exist.

Church writings going back as early as the second century
refer to the Gospel of Thomas; yet, no one in modern times ever
read the text until the discovery of ancient scrolls in the Nag
Hammadi region of Egypt in 1945. A local farmer was wandering
nearby cliffs searching for a naturally occurring fertilizer when he
accidentally came upon a cave containing some very old clay jars.
Once opened, these jars revealed thirteen leather-bound papyrus
manuscripts on which were written portions of fifty different texts.
Some are well-known Jewish and Christian scriptures—included
in the modern Bible—while others had been previously unknown
except through the references to them in other early writings.
There was even a copy of a passage from Plato's *Republic*! One of
the texts included in these ancient books was a full copy of the
Gospel of Thomas.

Many sayings recognizable from the canonical Gospels are
found in Thomas, although often with new meanings—even the
most well-known sayings, without their expected context or the
Gospel writers' ethical commentary, receive new hearings. Some
of the familiar parables are here, as well, although in such spare
form that they, too, sound fresh.

Most striking, however, are the sayings that are unique to this
Gospel. Thomas's Jesus is all ideas—many of which are not readily
comprehendable. Consider the following: "Lucky is the lion that
the human will eat, so that the lion becomes human. And foul is
the human that the lion will eat, and the lion still will become
human." "The dead are not alive, and the living will not die."
"Congratulations to the one who came into being before coming
into being." "When you make the two into one, and when you
make the inner like the outer and the outer like the inner, and
the upper like the lower . . . then you will enter [the Father's

domain]." This Gospel cries out for supplemental reference materials as does none of the others. You can't tune out while reading Thomas, expecting that you know what it's saying; to understand the Gospel of Thomas you must read actively and think carefully.

That you have to think about what you're reading is part of the excitement of Thomas. Reading these words, which many early Christians attributed to Jesus, it is easy to identify with those first believers who found his teachings strange and foreign. This is Christianity without centuries of tradition dictating a particular interpretation. Like the words of a Zen master's dharma talk, the teachings in Thomas are "dark to the mind yet radiant to the heart."

This Jesus speaks directly and powerfully to those who today would describe themselves as spiritual rather than religious. Thomas' Jesus is clearly not interested in founding a church. Consider Saying 3:

> Jesus said, "If those who lead you say to you, 'See, the kingdom is in the sky,' then the birds of the sky will precede you. If they say to you, 'It is in the sea,' then the fish will precede you. Rather, the kingdom is inside of you, and it is outside of you. When you come to know yourselves, then you will be known, and you will realize that it is you who are the sons of the living father."

It is true that in the canonical Gospels Jesus often attributes a miraculous healing to the faith of the person being healed rather than to some power of his own. Nowhere, however, is he clearer about the individual's own power and responsibility for her or his own spiritual life than in these words from Saying 70:

> If you bring forth what is within you, what is within you will save you. If you do not bring forth what is within you, what is within you will destroy you.

A Syrian tradition attributes the Gospel of Thomas to Didymos Judas Thomas, or Judas the twin, whom they hold to have been Jesus' twin brother. This claim can be traced back no earlier than a third-century work called the *Acts of Thomas*, and so is of questionable veracity. If they are correct, however, one could not ask for a more knowledgeable source.

Thomas is of little help in painting a picture of Jesus. Without stories, without a narrative structure through which to report his deeds, and without any kind of commentary to put these sayings into context—was he speaking a warning, a rebuke, a condemnation, or a teaching—knowing what to think of the man isn't easy. Yet for all of this Gospel's opacity, one exchange—one of the few things like a story to be found in the entire Gospel—seems to offer a completely believable portrait of the reaction this complex and compelling man engendered in his companions. That saying—Saying 13—seems an appropriate summation and ending to this part of our search:

> Jesus said to his disciples, "Compare me to something and tell me what I am like."
>
> Simon Peter said to him, "You are like a just angel."
>
> Matthew said to him, "You are like a wise philosopher."
>
> Thomas said to him, "Teacher, my mouth is utterly unable to say what you are like."

One Answer

He comes to us as One unknown, without a name, as of old, by the lake-side, He came to those men who knew Him not. He speaks to us the same word: "Follow thou me" and sets us to the tasks which He has to fulfill for our time. He commands. And to those who obey Him, whether they be wise or simple, He will reveal Himself in the toils, the conflicts, the sufferings, which they shall pass through in His fellowship, and, as an ineffable mystery, they shall learn in their own experience Who He is.

—Albert Schweitzer, *The Quest for the Historical Jesus*

JESUS PRESENTS A PROBLEM to the modern mind. How do we believe in a person when what we've been told about him is so unbelievable?

Leonard Bernstein composed a powerful theater piece for the opening of the Kennedy Center in Washington, DC. In one of the songs, various characters react to the Credo portion of the Catholic Mass. In response to the portion of the Apostle's Creed that talks about Jesus having been "made man" (*"et homo factus est"*), one of the characters sings,

And you became a man. You, God, chose to become a man. To
pay the earth a small social call. I tell you, sir, you never were a
man at all. Why? You had the choice when to live, when to
die, and then become a god again. . . .

You knew what you had to do. You knew why you had to
die. You chose to die and then revive again. You chose, you
rose, alive again. But I—I don't know why I should live if only
to die. Well I'm not going to buy it!

Many today feel that they're not able to "buy it" either. For
many, a primary stumbling block is the idea that this man named
Jesus was actually God, that he strode through life ultimately calling the shots and was, therefore, supremely confident of every
outcome. Such a Jesus has little to teach us; unlike him we wan-
der and stumble through life, unsure of how *anything* will turn
out. What could an all-knowing, all-powerful God-man teach us
about living our lives?

Another, more accessible way to understand the idea of Jesus'
divinity is to see his identification with God as so complete, their
relationship so intimate, that they seemed to be one and the same.
Jesus saw the world with God's eyes; he loved the world with God's
heart; and his acts were ultimately the acts of God. Those who looked
at Jesus saw God's face, and they met God directly through him. In
the second letter Paul wrote to the church in Corinth he says of
Jesus, "All the promises of God find their Yes in him." Yet none of
this meant that he could control the game any more than we can; he
just fully understood the rules. The Gospel of Luke tells us,

When the crowds learned [where Jesus was], they followed him;
and he welcomed them and spoke to them of the kingdom of
God, and cured those who had need of healing.

This passage contains four points that may tell us all we really
need to know about Yeshua ben Miriam. First, crowds of people

followed him. Something about Jesus—what he did, what he taught, who he was—drew people to him. The Gospels consistently tell us that people would not let Jesus alone; crowds followed him everywhere he went, seeking to be in his presence. And people are still seeking to follow him, even two thousand years after his death.

Second, Jesus welcomed these crowds. He welcomed not only the stereotypically "holy" or "righteous," but anyone who came to him. Each Gospel makes much of Jesus eating with "sinners," "tax collectors," and others that his society considered "unclean." Yet one may be particularly struck when reading Luke by how often Jesus was said to have eaten with Pharisees and Scribes! Everyone— anyone—who came to Jesus was welcomed; no one was turned away.

Third, Jesus "spoke of the kingdom of God." Jesus tried to teach people what God's rule, God's empire (basileia) was like. Jesus— with his unconditional welcome—formed a community that strove to be a living model of God's reign, God's kingdom, the Beloved Community where a seat at the "heavenly banquet" was offered to anyone who came. And Jesus was not merely just and good; in Bishop Spong's words, he was "God-intoxicated." Those who see Jesus as a fine moral example or as a gifted ethical teacher, yet who want to keep God out of the picture, miss a fundamental fact about this man. Wherever he went, in everything he did—not only in his words but in the living of his life—Jesus "spoke . . . of God." Stephen Patterson notes that the quest to know Jesus *is* the quest to know God; the two cannot be separated.

The fourth, and final, element in Luke's summation of Jesus' ministry is that he "cured those who had need of healing." In his lifetime Jesus was known as a healer. Many today have an acculturated skepticism about "faith healing" and may find this hard to accept, yet there is no way around it. Those who knew him, and even Jesus himself, acknowledged that his role as a healer was central to his overall ministry.

Yet, while not wanting to minimize at all the element of physical healing in Jesus' ministry, we should not limit our understanding of his healing work to bodily cures. In the Buddhist tradition, Siddhartha Gutama, who was called the Buddha, was also known as "the Great Doctor" and his teachings were called "medicine." In the Christian tradition, Jesus of Nazareth, who was called the Christ, was known to heal the body, mind, and soul of any who needed healing.

This is what one learns by searching scholarship and scripture; this is the picture that emerges. Still, the question posed so long ago is not "Who do *they* say that I am?" but "Who do *you* say that I am?" In other words, not "What do you understand?" but "What is our relationship?" And the question for us today, is: Can I still believe in Jesus even though I long ago gave up on fairy tales? Does it make sense, in the twenty-first century, to talk about having a relationship with a first-century religious teacher?

We can begin by acknowledging that Jesus must have been, first and foremost, a human being like any and every other human being who has ever lived. The difference was the depth of his faith/belief/trust in God, the intimacy of his relationship with the divine, and the clarity of his awareness. When he is remembered as saying, "The Father and I are one," he was talking about a union that is more clearly described with the words, "The Father is in me, and I am in the Father." The man we know as Jesus was so in touch with the sacred as to be as one with it, yet he was ever and always a man.

In my teens I listened to a song by the rock group Jethro Tull that begins,

> People what have you done? Locked him in his golden cage.
> Made him bend to your religion, Him resurrected from the grave.
> He is the god of nothing, if that's all that you can see. You are
> the god of everything. He's inside you and me. So lean upon

Him gently, but don't call on Him to save you from your social graces, and the sins you wish to waive.

Even with my understanding of who Jesus was, I have come to realize that I, too, am guilty of locking Jesus in that golden cage, effectively keeping him aloft and apart and making any real encounter impossible. Even though I had long ago rejected the high Christology and the traditional teachings from which the bars were formed, I nonetheless had kept the cage door securely locked. I now realize that when I turned away from the trappings of the tradition I had also turned my back on the figure trapped inside. To seek Jesus and have any hope of finding him required that I take him out of the gilded cage that hangs in the heavens and return him to earth. My first order of business was to unlock the door and invite Jesus back into my life.

If we look clearly at him we find a God-intoxicated man who offered others a living example of what it is to live in God's *basileia*, what it is to live *in* God. To see that example today one must dig through a great deal of tradition and interpretation by which he is obscured in the same way that centuries of dirt and soot obscured da Vinci's fresco of the Last Supper or Michelangelo's Sistine Chapel. Having grown up within the Christian tradition, I am very much aware of its faults and failings, yet I should not lose sight of its beauties and truths for all that. As I have reconnected with my Christian roots, I am moved by those who, without giving up their reason, gave over their hearts to this man from Nazareth; I have been reminded how I once gave my heart also, and have been led to wonder why I ever took it back.

For this man—like Siddhartha, like many saints and sages since—offers a Way. Interestingly, this was the name Jesus' followers first claimed for themselves—before they were "Christians" they were "people of the Way." In his life and teaching, even in the way his life and teaching are interpretively remembered in the Gospels, Jesus offered a vision and a challenge. Still, I do not believe that the call to "follow" is a call to worship the man who issued it. It is, instead, just what it appears to be: a call to follow him, to follow his path, to live as he lived. The author of the New Testament's *Letter to the Hebrews* calls Jesus, "the pioneer and perfector of our faith"; the catechism of the Hungarian Unitarian Christian Church refers to him as "the firstborn of the [children] of God."

One thing that stands out about Jesus—both as he is remembered in the scriptures and as he is rediscovered by the scholars— is his radical freedom. A story is told, with slight modifications, in all of the synoptic Gospels: A group comes to ask Jesus a question and begins by describing him in this way, "Teacher, we know that you are sincere, and show deference to no one; for you do not regard people with particularity, but teach the way of God in accordance with truth." Jesus lived a life in which the distinctions between rich and poor, holy and unholy, righteous and sinner, male and female, became increasingly meaningless. The lines of demarcation and division that we humans draw with ever greater clarity became invisible for this holy man. Looking at the world with God's eyes, he came to see all people as divine and all things as sacred; for him there were no distinctions. Reflecting on this aspect of Jesus, the apostle Paul wrote, "There is neither Jew nor Greek, there is neither slave nor free, there is neither male nor female; for you are all one in Christ Jesus." The life Jesus lived, the life he calls us to follow, is a life unbound by expectations— either of oneself or of others. The life Jesus lived, the life he calls us to follow, is a life that is truly, and in all ways, free.

And Jesus' example calls us to live in intimate union with the divine and with all that is. Bringing that union into greater manifestation—for oneself as well as for others—is understood to be of primary importance: "Seek first the kingdom of God, all else will follow." This is not merely an ethical path but a supremely spiritual one. It is a call to see the world as alive with divinity, ablaze with the sacred. As Ralph Waldo Emerson wrote in his Divinity School Address, "[Jesus] spoke of miracles; for he felt that man's life was miracle, and all that man doth. . . ."

There are, of course, consequences to living in such intimate union with the holy and sacred. A life so lived is a life in direct opposition to the values and mores of our "me first," acquisition-centered culture. It is a life that puts "success," as the world measures it, far down the list. It is a life that cannot accept the status quo, as long as current conditions keep anyone from reaching their full potential. Living such a life can be uncomfortable, unpopular, and is sure to be misunderstood. Yet none of the great teachers have invited us to travel easy roads, promising a journey without hindrances or dangers. Jesus is no exception. It is important to remember that he doesn't just call people to follow him, but to "pick up their own cross" and follow.

The life of the man named Jesus offers us an example, a model of how we can live, yet it also becomes clear that Jesus was and is more than an example. There were many holy men and healers in Jesus' day, as there have been many since. Yet something about *this* man has kept *his* name and *his* story alive for two thousand years. And Jesus is not just a remembered figure; for many today he is experienced as a living presence. In some way beyond comprehension, beyond facile explanations, the spirit of this God-intoxicated man lives on; and, if his life offers us an example, his living spirit offers us sustaining strength.

In fact, one might say that this is the heart of the Christian promise—that this man who lived in first-century Palestine, and in some mysterious way lives on, still welcomes all who respond to his call to follow, still points to a vision of God's rule made real, and still offers healing to those who have need. Creeds and catechism aside, this is the heart of Christian teaching. This is the permanent; all else is transient.

Yet this living spirit is not something that one can find in books. In the Gospel of John, Jesus is remembered as saying, "You search the scriptures because you think that in them you have eternal life . . . yet you refuse to come to me. . . ." This is what one finds in the searching, that Jesus continues to offer an invitation to every person to seek and find his or her own relationship with him—both the Jesus of history and the living spirit of Christ. Like any relationship, it will be different for every person, which is why the invitation is always individual and personal. And this is why Jesus' question always becomes personal as well: "Who do *you* say that I am?" In the end, the most important—and the most difficult—question of all turns out to be, "Can *I* believe? Am I able to? Am I willing to?"

Who Do You Say That I Am?

> History cannot prove that these things are true. One can only
> risk asserting that they are true, and listen and watch for this
> same God in one's own life. This is all the earliest Christians
> had to go on. It is all we have too. They understood that the
> resurrection of Jesus is a challenge . . . a call . . . an invitation.
> . . . This challenge, this call, this invitation are still ours today.
> —Stephen J. Patterson, *The God of Jesus*

THE SEARCH FOR JESUS—if it is to go beyond the merely academic
exploration—must always be personal. The guidance of a pastor
or priest, a scholar, or a fellow seeker is not as important as the
direction your own heart gives you. To be sure, such guides have
their places. Yet just as no travelogue describing a destination can
ever give you the experience that being there does, no church, no
creed, no catechism can give you the answer to the question, "Who
do *you* say that I am?"

A Jesuit priest was once asked how he was able to discern what
in the Bible was true and what was human invention. "I know Jesus,"
he said. "I have a relationship with the risen Christ, and I weigh
everything I read against my own experience of that relationship."

But how does one in the twenty-first century gain such a sense of experience? How do we, skeptical and cynical as so many of us are, even begin to explore something like a relationship with a person who lived and died two thousand years ago? Such a project seems to fly in the face of all that is sensible and rational.

There is a saying that to find God you must be willing to lose your mind. Mystics agree that reason is not the only way of knowing and that, in fact, too great a dependence on reason can hinder the spiritual search. Perhaps it would be more accurate, then, to say that you must be willing to *loose* your mind, to loosen the vice grip of the sensible and rational in order to allow the imaginative and intuitive ways of knowing to come to bear.

Let us begin by agreeing that to contemplate having a relationship with someone who died over two millennia ago *is* irrational. Just because it is irrational, however, does not mean that it is impossible, or that it is not worth your while. It simply means that your rational mind may not be the best tool to use. So what do you use? If you "lose your mind," what are you left with? Your imagination.

Try this experiment. Find a quiet, comfortable place to sit. It should be one that feels peaceful and will allow you to remain undisturbed for a while. Sit still. Close your eyes. Now call to mind an image of Jesus. It might be a picture you've seen in a children's Bible, or on TV, or in a movie. It might be something that pops into your mind without any obvious reference. Whatever the image is, wherever it comes from, allow yourself to linger with it, taking in all the details. Can you observe anything about the place where you see Jesus? Can you tell the time of day? The season? Bring the image to life, using all of your senses. Can you imagine sounds or smells? Place yourself in the scene. Can you feel the sun on your back or the wind in your hair? Be aware especially of how you feel inside—what are your emotional reactions, and how does Jesus "feel" to you?

Be very careful that you don't limit yourself to what you think you *ought* to experience in this exercise. Feeling anger, sorrow, or fear rather than the anticipated peace, love, and joy is not unusual. Especially for people who were raised in one of the Christian traditions and then walked away from it, pent-up emotions can surface. Remember, the whole point of this search is to discover for yourself your own experience, your own relationship with Jesus. So don't worry about who you think he's supposed to be and how you think others would expect you to act or feel in relation to him. Keep focused on what is actually there for you.

Now that you've called up an image of Jesus and tried to make it as real as your imagination can, is there anything you'd like to say to him? Is there anything he wants to say to you? Begin to engage Jesus in dialogue. This can feel very silly at first, and you might even wonder if there's any point to it. After all, aren't you just "making it up?" Actually, engaging in imaginative dialogue is a well-respected therapeutic technique in both dream work and several forms of counseling. Whether or not the entire content of the dialogue is coming from within your own mind is irrelevant; it can still have much to teach you. And most people who stay with this exercise over time report that they eventually notice elements in the dialogues that they feel certain do not come from within themselves, at least not from any conscious part. This is hard to explain, but is much clearer once experienced.

It is possible, of course, to carry on these conversations in your head, but recording the dialogues on paper, keeping a journal, allows you to look back, to notice the themes that arise and to explore areas of change and growth over time. You can do the exercise as described above, making written notes at the end, or you can begin writing after you have taken the time to bring the scene fully alive in your imagination, setting down the dialogue as it develops. Experiment to find what works best for you.

Do not hesitate to ask hard questions. "What was it like to have such a close relationship with the holy? What was it like to live with such an awareness of the sacred, to live as one with the divine? What was it like to hear that voice naming you a beloved son?" Or, from the other side, "Did you get scared? Did you feel overwhelmed? Did you doubt yourself, your abilities, and the sanity of the whole thing? Did you doubt your vision? Was it disappointing when they kept seeking signs, kept asking for miracles, when you were offering them life?" Ask whatever questions seem important to you and see what answers come.

A variation of this exercise is to use a story from one of the Gospels as the root image with which to interact. For example, you might use the story of Jesus calming the storm as told in the Gospel of Matthew (8:23–27):

> Then [Jesus] got into the boat and his disciples followed him. Without warning, a furious storm came up on the lake, so that the waves swept over the boat. But Jesus was sleeping. The disciples went and woke him, saying, "Lord, save us! We're going to drown!"
>
> He replied, "You of little faith, why are you so afraid?" Then he got up and rebuked the winds and the waves, and it was completely calm.
>
> The men were amazed and asked, "What kind of man is this? Even the winds and the waves obey him!"

Once more, sit still in a quiet place. Read over the story several times so that you know it well. Close your eyes and allow the scene to unfold in your imagination. Imagine yourself outside of the scene, observing, or as one of the characters, participating fully in the story. In either case, make the scene as real as possible in your mind. (Open your eyes to read again if you need to refresh your memory of the details.) Pay particular attention to what you're *feeling*—when you see the weather worsen, for instance, or when you notice that Jesus is sleeping while you are in fear for your life, or when Jesus rebukes the waves and they actually subside.

Some people find their imagination casting them in the role of Jesus and wonder whether that's acceptable. Of course it is! Explore what it feels like to be awakened from what might have been the first real sleep you've had in days. What are you feeling about these "men of little faith" who have been with you all this time and still don't seem to understand? What does it mean to you that the waves listen to your command?

After getting as deeply into the scene as your imagination will allow, see if the story will continue. What happens next? The Gospel writer jumps immediately to the boat's arrival at the other side of the lake. What happened in between? Did Jesus go back to sleep? Did the disciples talk among themselves? See whether details emerge in your mind's eye and then, as in the previous exercise, see whether you'd like to say anything to Jesus or whether he seems to want to say anything to you.

Or look at the story usually called "the woman caught in adultery" in the Gospel of John (8:1–11):

> Jesus went to the Mount of Olives. Early in the morning he came again to the temple; all the people came to him; and he sat down and taught them. The scribes and the Pharisees brought a woman who had been caught in adultery, and placing her in the midst they said to him, "Teacher, this woman has been caught in the act of adultery. Now in the law Moses commanded us to stone such. What do you say about her?" This they said to test him, that they might have some charge to bring against him. Jesus bent down and wrote with his finger on the ground. And as they continued to ask him, he stood up and said to them, "Let him who is without sin among you be the first to throw a stone at her." And once more he bent down and wrote with his finger on the ground. But when they heard

it, they went away, one by one, beginning with the eldest, and Jesus was left alone with the woman standing before him. Jesus looked up and said to her, "Woman, where are they? Has no one condemned you?" She said, "No one, Lord." And Jesus said, "Neither do I condemn you; go, and do not sin again."

Sit with this scene for a while. You might find yourself wondering, "What was going through your mind as the crowd surged forward, stones in hand, and that woman stepped backward in fear? What were you thinking when they asked you to decide?" Or, simply, "What were you writing in the sand?" Ask him! See what answers come.

Don't make the mistake of limiting your expectations of "dialogue" to the experience of a conversation with words. Instead, you might simply feel a warm sense of safety and security wash over you, or suddenly find yourself remembering a tumultuous time in your own life when the "wind and waves" seemed to suddenly subside (or didn't), or when it seemed that the crowds were getting ready to stone you. Such experiences can certainly be understood as part of a dialogue, communicating as surely as any words you might "hear." Such experiences, in fact, might be a much clearer, much more direct form of communication than words permit, considering how easily words can be misunderstood.

This kind of imaginative prayer exercise is often dismissed as some kind of "new age" fad or an overly psychological approach to spiritual matters. In fact, this exercise is drawn from a venerable part of the rich tradition of Christian prayer and contemplation, a tradition that has been largely lost over the centuries but is being resurrected in our day. This imaginative approach to prayer is actually based on a practice known as *lectio divina,* a divine reading of the scriptures in which one reads not for content but for illumination. Imagining oneself in the scripture story is a key to the practice.

Doing these exercises once or twice can be quite interesting and, just as when we examine the imagery of our dreams, can teach us a great deal. Engaging in this practice regularly, however, can transport you from an attempt to *understand* what is meant by having a relationship with Jesus to an actual *experience* of that relationship. From this place, you can answer the question, "Can I believe?" because from this place the question makes real sense. From this place—the place of experience—it is not hard to contemplate a relationship with someone who's been dead for two thousand years. You'll know it can be done because you will have done it.

So if you are serious about discovering or deepening this relationship, don't do this prayer practice once and then stop; instead, set some time aside each week—or, better yet, each day—to bring your whole self to it. Give yourself the space to really experience this relationship in and through your imagination. Bypass your rational mind's attempts to understand, and allow your imaginative mind to know. As with any relationship, the more time you spend on it and the more fully you share yourself, the deeper it will grow.

How will you know if anything is happening? How will you know whether or not what you experience is real or "just your imagination?" As recorded in the Gospel of John, Jesus concludes his final discourse with his disciples with the words, "These things I say to you that my joy may be in you and your joy may be complete." Joy—not simple happiness nor a hazy bliss, but deep, rich, complex joy—appears to be one of the unequivocal signs of a relationship with Jesus. So if you discover joy or any of the other "fruits of the Spirit"—peace, patience, kindness, goodness, faithfulness, gentleness, and self-control—increasing in your life, then it is likely that you have moved from "making it all up" to having a living relationship with Jesus, the living Christ.

We should keep in mind, however, a caution from the story of the Transfiguration (Luke 9:28–36), in which three of the dis-

ciples see Jesus suddenly surrounded by radiant light and conversing with Moses and Elijah. Afterward, those who witnessed the
event want to set up tents to mark the spot; their immediate reaction is to try to enshrine the experience. Jesus, however, rejects
this impulse. Centuries later the Christian mystic St. Theresa of
Avila would say that the greatest obstacle to an experience of God
is your last experience of God. Too many people—too many
churches—have turned the living Christ into a museum piece by
enshrining one experience, one encounter as if nothing before or
since could be as important. In so doing, they have effectively
closed their eyes to what *is* because of their devotion to what *was*.
Yet if there's one thing that the Christian and Hebrew scriptures
agree on about the divine it's that the God of Abraham, Isaac,
and Jacob—the God of Jesus—is always with us in the present
calling us into the future, not fossilized in the past. So, too, the
living Christ.

The Search Continues

If you venture to wonder how Christ would have looked if he had shaved and had his hair cut . . . or whether he swore when he stood on a nail in the carpenter's shop . . . or whether he laughed over the repartees by which he baffled the priests . . . you will produce an extraordinary dismay and horror among the iconolaters. You will have made the picture come out of its frame, the statue descend from its pedestal, the story become real, with all the incalculable consequences that may flow from this terrifying miracle.

—George Bernard Shaw, *Androcles and the Lion*

THE JESUS WE MEET on our spiritual quest—and the God we meet in and through him—is not a moldy museum piece but a living reality. Like any other, a relationship with Jesus takes both *attention* and *intention*. A seventeenth-century French monk, known to us as Brother Lawrence, encouraged his brothers to apply the same standard to their relationship with God, with Christ, as they would to any human relationship: "Are we not rude and deserve blame, if we leave Him alone to busy ourselves about trifles, which do not please Him, and perhaps offend him?" In other words, if you claim to want a friendship with someone but never call or visit, what would your potential friend assume about the sincerity of your desire? Or, what if you went to visit this friend but spent the whole time doing something else and ignoring her or him, what would that say about the depth of your friendship?

If we are seriously seeking a relationship with Jesus Christ, we must be mindful that such a relationship will not be a one-sided affair. If it is real, it will not be wholly up to us—a real relationship makes its own demands. And we have seen the kinds of demands Jesus makes. We have heard the call he issued during his lifetime and which he issues still to those who seek him today. "Follow me," he says. "Take seriously what I took seriously. Make real God's *basileia*. Do this in remembrance of me."

This is not for the fainthearted.

There are two dangers that easily befall people seeking a relationship with Jesus. The first is the tendency to end up worshiping him. We should remember the words of Ralph Waldo Emerson: "Is it not time to present this matter of Christianity exactly as it is, to take away all false reverence for Jesus, and not mistake the stream for the source?" Jesus himself kept directing people's attention toward God as the proper locus of their devotion (except, as noted, as remembered in the Gospel of John). Shouldn't we do the same? "Why do you call me good?" he asked. "No one is good but God alone."

The Jesus we've met on this journey was not—is not—God, even if we can see God in and through him. A doorway is not the room to which it gives access; a window is not the view it provides. Jesus is a door, a window, a conduit to and for the holy. He is an *icon* to look through, not an *idol* to look at for its own sake. Yeshua ben Miriam was a man so in touch with God himself that he presented a vision of the divine to those who could see him clearly. Not everyone could, and not everyone can today. But to those who "have eyes to see" the living spirit of Jesus provides a way to conceive the inconceivable and to imagine what is beyond our imagining. God is utterly beyond our comprehension, but Jesus offers a picture of God in human form.

It is understandable that people conflate the two, that many have mistaken "the stream for the source," and, in the words of a well-known Zen parable, confused the finger that points at the moon for the moon itself. That this is understandable does not make it any less of an error, however. A relationship with Jesus ought not be the end, in and of itself, of our searching. Just as it was for those who knew him best, the relationship with Jesus provides an entrée to a relationship with God. As Stephen Patterson noted, the search for Jesus is the search for God and this should be our end.

So why, then, look to Jesus at all? Why not turn our eyes directly to God and refuse to deal with any kind of "middle man"? It is a human tendency to think of the general in terms of the particular. If someone says "nature," most of us conjure up images of specific places in nature we have known and loved. If someone says "music," we begin to hear our favorite songs. If someone says "academic" or "minister," we call to mind those professors and clergy persons we either admired or despised. It is human nature for us to think in particular examples rather than abstract generalizations.

God is a word that attempts to convey a reality much larger than nature or music or minister. How much more, then, might we benefit from a concrete image? Through Jesus' example of love, we can conceive of God's inconceivable love; through his model of openness and acceptance, we can imagine the unimaginable breadth of God's welcome. Jesus, for those who see him clearly, can be a window through which we can see God; a frame that allows us to focus on a reality far beyond our ability to grasp.

The second danger that befalls those seeking a relationship with Jesus can be found in what some refer to as "Jesus is my friend" Christianity which, at its worst, can create a sugarcoated worldview, a Pollyanna perspective from which everything takes on a rosy glow because "Jesus is my friend." This kind of Christianity reverences the Sunday School Jesus—the calm, impassive, perfect, detached God-man—and emphasizes that we are all children of God and can be as happy and carefree as children if only we have Jesus as our friend. After all, as the song says, "Jesus loves the little children."

But Jesus does not call us to be children. He calls us to be women and men of God. He calls us to a mature relationship, not a paternalistic and protected second childhood. Just look again at the stories recorded in the Christian scriptures. Does everything look rosy in the lives of those who knew him best? Were the disciples immune to pain and fear, to stresses and strife? Did their friendship with Jesus make them untroubled, happy-go-lucky, with a song in their hearts and a smile on their lips? If anything, their relationship with Jesus seems to have made their lives harder. Isn't Jesus remembered as saying that he did not come to bring peace but, rather, a sword?

This is a far cry from the blissful serenity of the "Jesus is my friend" people. Yet if we are serious about seeking a relationship with Jesus, we must be clear not only about *whom* we are seeking, but also about *what* we are seeking. A real relationship requires a real "other"—someone who is not me and who will not always live up to my expectations or fit into the mold of my assumptions. If our relationship with Jesus is to be real, it must be predicated on our recognition that Jesus is real—it will not be all up to us. Somehow beyond our understanding—but evidenced in experience—the spirit of that young man who lived so long ago lives still, and he will have a say in how our relationship unfolds. Again, this might not make rational sense, but as countless witnesses throughout time attest, it makes experiential sense. If our relationship with Jesus is to be a real one, we must be open to his continuing reality.

This means that we must remain open to the possibility of being surprised. This is because real relationships are never static, unchanging, set, and settled; they are always evolving, as the people involved grow and change. A real relationship is a process of discovery. I react to my friend and my friend reacts to me, and each of us is changed in the process.

And, so, in the end, our search for Jesus can never be finished. For if the Jesus we seek is indeed the living Christ—and not just a tradition's enshrined memory or our own expectant projection— then the Jesus we find today is not the same Jesus we'll find tomorrow. We must always keep looking. Yet Jesus himself gives us hope. In the Gospel of Thomas (77:2–3) he is remembered as saying, "Split a piece of wood; I am there. Lift up the stone, and you will find me there." He is also remembered as assuring his companions, in the words that conclude the Gospel of Matthew (28:20), "I am with you always, to the very end of the age."

Notes

The Secular World

"'. . . a citizen of our century at the same time.'" p. 3: John Shelby Spong, *Why Christianity Must Change or Die* (San Francisco: HarperSanFrancisco, 1998), p. 18.

"'. . . God send us a real religious life.'" p. 4: Conrad Wright, ed., *Three Prophets of Liberal Religion* (Boston: Beacon Press, 1961), p. 121, 145, 146.

Modern Views

"'. . . through a revelation of Jesus Christ.'" p. 8: Galatians 1:11–12.

". . . written down until about 60 C.E." p. 8: Modern scholars frequently use the initials "B.C.E." and "C.E." to refer, respectively, to "before the Common Era" and "Common Era." These designations replace the more familiar "B.C." and "A.D.," which refer to "before Christ" and "Anno Domini" ("in the year of our Lord"), which are now understood to reflect a Christian bias.

"'. . . roguery of others of his disciples.'" p. 9: Letter to William Short, quoted in Stephen Mitchell, *The Gospel According to Jesus* (New York: HarperPerennial, 1993), p. 281. This project eventually resulted in what is known today as *The Jefferson Bible*, published by Beacon Press.

"'. . . a sound human mind can love any person.'" p. 11: Passages from Emerson's journals quoted in ibid., pp. 285–286.

"'. . . prove transient also.'" p. 12: Sermon delivered at the ordination of Rev. Charles C. Shackford on May 19, 1841, and reprinted in Wright, *Three Prophets*, pp. 113–149.

"'. . . what never existed at his time?'" p. 13: John Dominic Crossan, *Jesus: A Revolutionary Biography* (San Francisco: HarperSanFrancisco, 1994), p. xii.

"'. . . *a Jesus entirely congenial to you.*'" p. 14: Robert Funk and Roy Hoover, *The Five Gospels* (New York: Macmillan, 1993), p. 5.

"'. . . I have come not to abolish but to fulfill.'" p. 14: Matthew 5:17. The Jesus Seminar does not consider this to be an authentic saying of Jesus because it can be seen as addressing too coincidentally a doctrinal difficulty of the early church. Still, it reflects Jesus' sense of himself as one seeking to renew or revive his own tradition. See Marcus Borg, *Jesus: A New Vision* (San Francisco: Harper & Row, 1987), and Spong, *This Hebrew Lord*, for more.

". . . Second Isaiah's 'suffering servant,'. . . ." p. 15: This is a passage from the Hebrew Scriptures that has often been used by Christians as a description of Jesus, "He is despised and rejected of men; a man of sorrows, and acquainted with grief; and we hid as it were our faces from him; he was despised and we esteemed him not. Surely he hath borne our griefs, and carried our sorrows; yet we did esteem him stricken, smitten of God, and afflicted." Isaiah 53:3f.

". . . conflicting messages into his mouth." p. 15: For more, see Borg, *Jesus*, and Stephen J. Patterson, *The God of Jesus* (Harrisburg: Trinity Press, 1998).

"'. . . out of places like Palestine.'" p. 15: Patterson, *The God of Jesus*, p. 63.

"'. . . the son of Mary?'" p. 16: Mark 6:3.

". . . executed by Rome as a political criminal." p. 18: Crucifixion was a means of execution employed by Rome in cases of crimes against the state. If Jesus was being punished for religious crimes, it seems unlikely that the Romans would have crucified him. See Crossan, *Jesus*.

Ancient Visions

". . . written by others and put into his mouth." p. 19: Robert Funk and Roy Hoover, *The Five Gospels* (New York: Macmillan, 1993).

". . . in the preparation of their own Gospels." p. 21: For more information, see Funk and Hoover, *The Five Gospels*.

". . . and John somewhere around 100 C.E." p. 22: For convenience, the Gospels are often referred to by the name of the author to whom they are ascribed.

The Gospel of Mark

". . . who is mentioned in the Book of Acts." p. 23: See Acts 12:12 and 15:37.

"'. . . with you I am well pleased.'" p. 23: Mark 1:1.

"'. . . for they were afraid.'" p. 23: Mark 16:8. The story of the Easter encounter is Mark 16:1–7, and the suspicious post-resurrection material is found in Mark 16:9–20.

"Although Mark's Jesus says he came to preach . . . ." p. 23: See Mark 2:38.

". . . to say nothing to anyone about it." p. 24: These references are, in turn, Mark 1:24, 5:7, 8:30, and 9:2–9.

"'. . . but not understand.'" p. 24: Mark 4:12. This phrase is reminiscent of Isaiah 6:9–10, "Make the heart of this people fat, and their ears heavy, and shut their eyes; lest they see with their eyes, and hear with their ears, and understand with their hearts, and turn and be healed."

". . . one of which they have just experienced together." p. 24: The two feedings can be found in Mark 6:34–44 and 8:1–10. Jesus' frustration is expressed in Mark 8:17–21.

". . . fed a group of one hundred with only twenty loaves of bread?" p. 25: 2 Kings 4:42–44.

The Gospel of Matthew

". . . a tax collector who was also known as 'Levi.'" p. 25: See Matthew 9:9–13, Mark 2:13–17, Luke 5:27–32.

". . . understood as the fulfillment of prophecy." p. 26: Isaiah 7:14.

". . . away from their bondage to sin." p. 27: For more, see Spong, *This Hebrew Lord.*

". . . his disciples are to go out to 'all the nations.'" p. 28: See Matthew 10:1–7 for the former position, and Matthew 28:19 for the latter.

". . . asking him to heal her daughter." p. 28: The whole story can be seen at Matthew 15:21–28.

The Gospel of Luke

". . . mentioned in several of Paul's epistles." p. 29: See Col. 4:14, 2 Tim. 4:11, and Philem. 24.

"'. . . concerning the things of which you have been informed.'" p. 29: Luke 1:1–5.

". . . during their pregnancies." p. 29: Luke 1:5–80. For the interaction between Mary and Elizabeth, see Luke 1:39–56.

"'. . . I had to be in my Father's house?'" p. 30: Luke 2:41–52.

"'. . . and cured those who had need of healing.'" p. 30: Luke 9:11.

". . . talking with Jesus—after his death." p. 30: Luke 24:13–32.

The Gospel of John

". . . said to be written by the disciple John. . . . " p. 31: See Matthew 10:2. This is one of a number of specific references in the Gospels to the disciple John.

"'. . . and the life was the light of men.'" p. 31: John 1:1–5.

". . . who has come down to fulfill a specific mission." p. 32: See, for instance, John 8:23.

"'. . . and the truth, and the life.'" p. 32: These references are, respectively, John 4:7–15, 6:35, 8:12, 15:5, and 10:11. It is undoubtedly not coincidental that the phrase "I am," used over and over by Jesus in John, is the reply Yahweh gave to Moses when asked for a name—"Tell them I AM has sent you." (Exodus 3:14).

". . . he inspires an exciting vision indeed." p. 33: These references are, respectively, John 14:18, 20; 14:12; and 15:11.

The Gospel of Thomas

"'. . . then you will enter [the Father's domain].'" p. 34: In order, these references are Thomas 7; 11:2; 19:1; and 22:4, 7.

One Answer

"'. . . and then become a god again. . . .'" p. 38: Non-Credo from Bernstein's Mass.

"'. . . find their Yes in him.'" p. 38: 2 Corinthians 1:20.

"'. . . and cured those who had need of healing.'" p. 38: Luke 9:11.

"'. . . and I am in the Father.'" p. 40: John 10:30 and 10:38.

"'. . . and the sins you wish to waive.'" p. 41: "My God" on Jethro Tull's Aqualung.

". . . 'the firstborn of the [children] of God.'" p. 42: The quote from St. Paul can be found in Hebrews 12:2. For the Hungarian Unitarian teachings on Jesus see Andráshi, György (trans.), "Hungarian Unitarian Catechism: The Catechism of the Hungarian Unitarian Church in Transylvanian Romania," The Unitarian Universalist Christian, Volume 49, Nos. 3–4 Fall/Winter 1994.

"'. . . but teach the way of God in accordance with truth.'" p. 42: Mark 12:14.

"'. . . for you are all one in Christ Jesus.'" p. 42: Galatians 3:28.

"'. . . all else will follow.'" p. 42: Matthew 6:33.

"'. . . yet you refuse to come to me . . . .'" p. 44: John 5:39–40.

Who Do You Say That I Am?

"... not for content but for illumination." p. 50: For more on *lectio divina* see Thelma Hall, *Too Deep for Words: Rediscovering Lectio Divina* (New York: Paulist Press, 1988) or Martin Smith, *The Word Is Very Near You* (Cambridge, MA: Cowley Publications, 1989).

"... faithfulness, gentleness, and self-control ...." p. 51: Galatians 5:22–23.

The Search Continues

"'... which do not please him, and perhaps offend him?'" p. 53: Brother Lawrence, *The Practice of the Presence of God* (London: A. R. Mowbray & Co. Limited, 1954), pp. 83–84.

"'... and not mistake the stream for the source?'" p. 54: Passages from Emerson's journals quoted in Stephen Mitchell, *The Gospel According to Jesus* (New York: HarperPerennial, 1993), p. 281.

"... 'No one is good but God alone.'" p. 54: Luke 18:18–19.

"... he did not come to bring peace but, rather, a sword?" p. 56: Matthew 10:34.

Resources for the Search

Books

The Bible. The New Oxford Annotated Bible with the Apocrypha, Revised Standard Version. New York: Oxford University Press, 1977. There are, of course, many translations of the Bible, but the revised standard version is considered one of the most accurate, and the annotations make this a dream for studying.

Borg, Marcus. *Jesus: A New Vision: Spirit, Culture, and the Life of Discipleship*. San Francisco: Harper & Row, 1987. A very accessible book by a well-known Jesus scholar that attempts to reconstruct the life of Jesus. The first section deals with "Jesus and the Spirit" and the second with "Jesus and Culture."

———. *Meeting Jesus Again for the First Time*. San Francisco: HarperSanFrancisco, 1994. The title says it all. A very exciting (re)introduction to this remarkable figure by a remarkable scholar.

Breech, James. *The Silence of Jesus: The Authentic Voice of the Historical Man*. Philadelphia: Fortress Press, 1983. Dr. Breech, a professor of New Testament studies, examines eight sayings and twelve parables which virtually all scholars agree are authentic to Jesus, asking what these words can tell us about the man who uttered them. Breathes new life into the well-known words.

Buechner, Frederick. *Faces of Jesus*. San Francisco: Harper & Row, 1974. A beautiful meditation in words and pictures on the many ways Jesus has been depicted throughout the centuries. Buechner's prose is as lovely as the paintings.

Crossan, John Dominic. *Jesus: A Revolutionary Biography*. San Francisco: HarperSanFrancisco, 1994. In 1991 Crossan published the ground-breaking *The Historical Jesus: The Life of a Mediterranean Jewish Peasant*. It was considered a critical success, but far too long and academic for the average lay person to plow through. This is a more "popular" version of that more extensive work.

de Mello, Anthony. *Sadhana: Christian Exercises in Eastern Form*. Liguori: Ligouri/Triumph, 1978. This Catholic monk who was raised in India offers one hundred imaginative prayer exercises. A veritable (and venerable) "how to" book for this approach to prayer.

Driver, Tom. *Christ in a Changing World*. New York: Crossroad, 1981. Driver takes aim at many of the traditional teachings of the church about Christ and develops a Christology for the modern age. One of the most exciting books on Christology in recent years.

Fox, Matthew. *The Coming of the Cosmic Christ*. San Francisco: Harper & Row, 1988. Profound theologian Matthew Fox, director of the Institute in Culture and Creation Spirituality, argues for a shift away from a focus on the historic incarnation of Christ in Jesus so that we might turn our attention to the ongoing "Cosmic Christ," which he sees as the only real hope for healing our wounded world.

Funk, Robert, and Roy Hoover. *The Five Gospels: What Did Jesus Really Say?* Santa Rosa, CA: Polebridge Press, 1993. A summary of the work to date of the group of scholars known as the Jesus

Seminar. They have done a new translation of the Gospels of Matthew, Mark, Luke, John, and Thomas—with an ear toward rendering the style as well as the content of the original Greek texts—and have color-coded the sayings attributed to Jesus to reflect their assessment of the probable authenticity of the attribution. There is also a very interesting overview of methods of New Testament study.

Kazantzakis, Nikos. *The Last Temptation of Christ.* New York: Simon & Schuster, 1960. A powerfully evocative and challenging version of Jesus' life. Here we find a very human Jesus, one who isn't so sure he wants to be Messiah. Kazantzakis' reflections offer much to think about.

Lawrence, Brother. *The Practice of the Presence of God.* London: A. R. Mowbray & Co. Ltd., 1954. Contains four "conversations" and fifteen letters expanding on this humble monk's practice of living in the ongoing presence of God. Simple, yet far from simplistic, this book offers a vivid portrait of one who took the idea of a relationship with Christ and made it a reality in his life.

Marxsen, Willi. *Jesus and the Church: The Beginnings of Christianity.* Philadelphia: Trinity Press International, 1992. This collection of essays can be a little tough to follow, but it is a fascinating glimpse into the level of debate that has arisen concerning the question "who was/is Jesus?" The discussions of whether the historical figure of Jesus has any relevance for Christianity, whether Jesus was merely the bearer of the Gospel or the content of the Gospel, and whether Christianity can be said to have begun only after Jesus' lifetime will be revelations to those who perceive the Christian tradition as either simplistic or monolithic.

Mitchell, Stephen. *The Gospel According to Jesus.* New York: HarperPerennial, 1993. Stephen Mitchell is a translator of sacred material who has a fine ear and an open heart. Here he turns to

the Gospels and, following the pattern established by Thomas
Jefferson, attempts to tease out of the four Gospels a single story.
Bringing to bear research done by scholars in the field of Jesus
study as well as his own understanding of spiritual masters, this is
a very intriguing reconstruction.

Patterson, Stephen J. *The God of Jesus: The Historical Jesus and the
Search for Meaning*. Harrisburg: Trinity Press, 1998. Patterson, a
member of the Jesus Seminar, has attempted to bring together two
previously separate goals—the search for what can be known about
the historical figure of Jesus (the historian's goal), and the search
for the meaning to be found in this figure (the theologian's goal).

Peterson, Eugene. *The Message: The New Testament, Psalms, and
Proverbs in Contemporary Language*. Colorado Springs: NavPress,
1993. Peterson has rendered a new translation in an attempt to be
both accurate and evocative. His translations of the Epistles, especially, are vibrant with life.

Saramago, José. *The Gospel According to Jesus Christ*. New York:
Harcourt Brace, 1994. A poetic, and at times surreal, retelling of the
story of Jesus' life by this Portuguese Nobel Prize–winning novelist.

Spong, John Shelby. *This Hebrew Lord*. San Francisco:
HarperSanFrancisco, 1974. An early book by Spong, the focus is
on Jesus as Jew, reclaiming his Hebrew identity and putting him
once again in his proper lineage. Several chapters try to give a
more modern interpretation—using the metaphor of *Jonathan
Livingston Seagull*, for instance.

———. *Why Christianity Must Change or Die: A Bishop Speaks to
Believers in Exile*. San Francisco: HarperSanFrancisco, 1998. Analysis
of why the Christian church is in need of change and what steps
might be taken to change it. An exciting and challenging book.

————. *A New Christianity for a New World: Why Traditional Faith Is Dying and How a New Faith Is Being Born*. San Francisco: HarperSanFrancisco, 2001. This is a continuation of the work he began in *Why Christianity Must Change or Die*. He goes further than ever before in describing what this "new faith" will look like.

Wilson, A. N. *Jesus: A Life*. New York: W. W. Norton, 1992. Wilson is not a New Testament scholar but a noted biographer, having written works on Tolstoy and C. S. Lewis. This book introduces some very provocative ideas and, while some of them lack solid support, the challenge they offer to think in new ways is exciting.

Wright, Conrad, ed. *Three Prophets of Religious Liberalism: Channing, Emerson, Parker*. Boston: Skinner House, 1996. Collecting Ralph Waldo Emerson's "Divinity School Address," William Ellery Channing's "Unitarian Christianity," and Theodore Parker's "The Transient and Permanent in Christianity," this volume is a rich resource for anyone looking into the history of Unitarian Christianity. The ideas expressed in these sermons are refreshing even today.

Music

Bernstein, Leonard. *Mass: A Theater Piece for Singers, Musicians, and Dancers*. Sony Classics, 1997. While not specifically about Jesus, this is a powerful meditation on the role of faith in the modern world and contains moving and wonderful expressions of the reaction many women and men have had, and continue to have, to traditional church teachings.

Schwartz, Steven. *Godspell: A Musical Based upon the Gospel According to St. Matthew*. Original Off-Off-Broadway Cast Recording, BMG/Arista, 1974. This is a retelling of the Gospel stories (drawing heavily on the Gospel of Matthew), full of flash and fun. It could only have come into being in the '60s.

Weber and Rice. *Jesus Christ Superstar*. Original Cast Recording, UCI/MCA, 1970. The classic "rock opera" that was attacked by fundamentalists and embraced by liberals.

Videos

Arcand, Denys. *Jesus of Montreal* (Orion Pictures Corp., 1990). The story of Jesus is woven through the story of a theatre troupe attempting to stage a somewhat avant-garde passion play. Very powerful.

Greene, David. *Jesus Christ Superstar* (Universal Studios, 1973). The film version of the rock opera mixes ancient settings with modern (1960s) images to create a somewhat surreal yet powerfully moving experience.

Jewison, Norman. *Godspell* (Columbia Tristar, 1973). This film captures the spirit of the stage version of this show. It's dated, but delightful.

Scorsese, Martin. *The Last Temptation of Christ* (Universal City Studios, Inc., 1988). Many lined up to condemn this film, a passable adaptation of Nikos Kazantzakis' book by the same name. This is the story of a very human Jesus, which was the source of the movie's controversy. If you don't have the time to read the book, see the movie.

Zeffirelli, Franco. *Jesus of Nazareth* (RAI/ITC Entertainment, Inc., 1977). A six-and-a-half-hour telling of the life of Jesus, originally broadcast on television during Easter week, this beautifully evocative film is quite moving.

Web Sites

Beliefnet (www.beliefnet.com)
This brings you to the index for the discussion section of Beliefnet. Click on the link for "Christianity: Progressive" and you will be able to join with other liberal and progressive Christians.

Christianity for the Third Millennium (www.intac.com/~rollins/ctm.html)
C.T.M. has been formed by Christians who believe that contemporary biblical and historical scholarship can and should become an integral part of the basis of their faith in Jesus Christ. They believe that only a conscientious reexamination of the Christian symbols will enable their cherished faith tradition to survive into the third millennium. This site is affiliated with Bishop John Shelby Spong.

The Center for Progressive Christianity (www.tcpc.org)
The Center is for people who "find more grace in the search for meaning than in absolute certainty, in the questions rather than in the answers" and "have religious interests and longings but cannot accept the beliefs and dogmas you associate with Christianity [and are] repelled by claims that Christianity is the 'only way.'"

Christian Image Link Source (www.laughingjesus.50megs.com)
Self-proclaimed "World's largest collection of Jesus Christ images," this non-denominational site provides links to literally hundreds of artists' renditions of Jesus.

The Face: Jesus in Art (www.thefaceonline.org)
This is the online version of the 2001 PBS documentary looking at the way Jesus has been depicted through the centuries in art around the world.

Jesus of the Week (www.jesusoftheweek.com)
If you're stuck with the "cardboard cutout," Sunday School image of Jesus, this site is for you. An unusual collection of (mostly kitsch) depictions of Jesus, accompanied by tremendously irreverent commentary.

Sacred Space (www/Jesuit.ie/prayer)
This site, run by the Irish Jesuits, provides gentle guidance through the prayer form known as *lectio divina*.

The Sophia Center (www.sophiacenter.net)
This "reflective oasis in cyberspace" provides an interfaith forum exploring whether it is possible to be genuinely contemporary and religious at the same time.

Unitarian Universalist Christian Fellowship (www.uua.org/uucf)
This site is dedicated to promoting Christianity within the Unitarian Universalist movement as well as offering a progressive vision to the wider Christian community. This site provides links to important Unitarian and Universalist writings, as well as to other progressive Christian communities.

University of Creation Spirituality (www.creationspirituality.com)
Started by Matthew Fox, an ex-Catholic (now Episcopal) priest, UCS is a haven for those who have a broad, inclusive, Creation-centered understanding of the Christian tradition.

Acknowledgments

I am a practicing preacher, so I work with words quite a bit—counting newsletter columns and sermons, I write some 94,000 words a year. Yet nothing I have done before prepared me for the work of writing a book. The thirteenth-century Christian mystic Meister Echardt once said that if you can manage only one prayer in your life, and it is "thank you," it will be sufficient.

As I sit down to write acknowledgments for this, my first book, I feel something like those first-time Academy Award winners who try breathlessly to thank anyone and everyone they've ever known. I would like to begin my litany of thanksgiving by thanking that ineffable mystery that is known by so many names yet is by no name fully known—I would like to thank that which I call God, from whom all good things truly flow. In my life there are many good things. I would also like to thank the ongoing, living spirit of Jesus, my constant companion on this journey (even when I didn't know or believe it).

And then there are so many people I would like to thank, so many people who have helped shape my thinking, without whom I would not have become the minister, or the man, I am today. Although I want to place no responsibility on them for the thoughts expressed here, I do hope that they will read these words with pleasure and find in them familiar echoes of the things they taught me.

- Rev. Ed Lane and the people of the First Parish Universalist Unitarian Church of Waltham, Massachusetts: you gave me a home.
- Rev. Nancy Campbell and the people of the First Parish Church of Lincoln, Massachusetts: you gave me roots.
- Rev. Gary E. Smith and the people of First Parish in Concord, Massachusetts, Unitarian Universalist: you taught me to fly.
- The faculty of the Shalem Institute for Spiritual Formation and the members of the Spiritual Guidance Program (Winter Residency Class of 2001): you lit the fire.
- The people of the First Universalist Church of Yarmouth, Maine: you helped me to grow.
- Mary Brand-James, with whom I am privileged to travel on the journey of this life: you make everything else possible.

I'd like to give thanks to my father, Walter Wikstrom, for reading the first draft of the summer study project that formed the basis of this book and giving me consistent encouragement through its multiple revisions, and to Lisa Perkins, whose editorial expertise helped make the dream of this book a reality. (She returned my manuscript covered in so many notes that at times it was hard to find my original words! This turned out to be a good thing, for all of her suggestions were improvements.) I have deep gratitude, also, for Bishop John Shelby Spong and his willingness to read an unsolicited (and unpolished!) manuscript and offer prompt and insightful assistance.

I would also like to thank the folks at Skinner House Books—Joni McDonald, Betsy Martin, Kristen Radloff, Patricia Frevert, Suzanne Morgan, and especially Mary Benard—for all of their help in turning this manuscript into a book and this writer into an author.

Thanks also to colleagues and friends who have walked with me as I've wrestled with my faith: the Reverends Mark Monson Alley, Rev. Karen Brammer, Barbara Brand-James, Tom Cushman, Steve Jones Goldstein, Loraine Giles, Scott Hamilton, David Heald, Bryan Jessup, K. Karpen, Carol Meyer, Rick Ochsner, Nurya Love Parish, Peter Plagge, Paul Rasor, Jill Saxby, Gary Smith, and Dale Winter. Thanks also, of course, to the people of the First Universalist Church of Yarmouth, with whom I have had the privilege and pleasure of serving as minister since 1995. The great gift of Unitarian Universalism, and of this congregation in particular, is the freedom to search within the full spectrum of religious possibilities, to seek Truth in whatever form(s) it takes, to listen to the still, small voice of the divine in all of the languages it knows and loves. For this freedom I am grateful; without this freedom, this book would not be possible.

And finally, as the orchestra begins to play telling me that it's time to wrap up the "thank you" speech, I'd like to acknowledge some of the authors who have particularly influenced my thinking. I have never met these people, yet I have spent much time with them over the years: Martin Bell, Frederich Buechner, Tom Driver, Thich Nhat Hanh, Henri Nouwen, and Bishop John Shelby Spong. It was they who nurtured the seed in me of becoming a writer that my parents long ago planted.

Thank you all.

Rev. Erik Walker Wikstrom

September, 2003